MIND

GONE

WILD

FINDING FREEDOM WITHIN THE CHAOS

MW01228089

MIND GONE WILD

FINDING FREEDOM WITHIN THE CHAOS

ALLAN KNIGHT M.Ed.

Mind Gone Wild by Allan Knight
Copyright © 2018 Allan Knight. All Rights Reserved.

All rights reserved. No part of this publication may be reproduced stored in a retrieval system or transmitted in any form or by any means – electronic, mechanical, photocopying, and recording or otherwise – without the prior written permission of the author, except for brief passages quoted by a reviewer or by another author in which the quote is fully attributed. To perform any of the above, other than the exceptions, is an infringement of copyright law.

ISBN: 978-0-9877385-9-2

Liability Disclaimer: The author and publisher disclaim all liability arising from the usage of advice in this book. If professional assistance is required, a competent professional should be consulted. This book does not constitute professional advice and is not a replacement for a live consultation.

Front Cover Art and Design by: sddesigns

Edition: April 2018

Acknowledgements

This book is dedicated to the amazing people I have been so fortunate to know and learn from throughout my life:

To my late dear soul mate, Suzie, who continues to be the joy of my life even after her passing. Because of her, I have a greater sense of unconditional love. I learned from her the importance of integrity, personal awareness and the art of listening. I love her so deeply and continue to benefit from her support and guidance.

To Stefan, my closest friend for over thirty-five years. Without his support and wisdom, there is no way I would be where I am today. Most of all, he taught me the importance of true friendship.

To my dear friend Joanne, one of the wisest women I know. Through her wisdom, intuition and advice over the years, I have a better understanding of women and relationships; mostly importantly, the relationship I have with myself.

To my brother, Larry, who has truly been an extraordinary role model and has blessed my life with his huge heart, amazing intelligence and love for life.

To my late business partner Stephen, who called himself my "tor-mentor". His passion, determination, focus and attention to detail helped me to become a much more determined person, and for that I am most grateful.

To Bobby, a special friend for over 30 years who is the most loyal and honest person I know. Not only is he extremely wise, but his sense of humor has helped me stay grounded and not take life so seriously.

To my friend Henry who passed away last year, who taught me the importance of hard work, determination and self-responsibility. His success story is an inspiration to us all.

To Claude who has provided great friendship over the years and above all else, made me laugh more than anyone I know.

To Dean Martin, in my estimation, the greatest TV personality of all time. Thank you for teaching me the importance of having a fun loving spirit and joy for life. Thank you also for your contributions on the internet where thousands of people around the world can still see you and 'feel good'.

To all my friends and acquaintances who have contributed in so many ways to my professional and personal growth. I am truly grateful and can surely say that without you this book would never have been written.

Contents

MIND GONE WILD

PART 1

Introduction

Every day my morning walk has a similar feel. It all starts out with a sense of gratitude for being alive, for the people in my life, for things I have and the opportunities that have come way. I am even grateful for the challenges I have faced as they always provide me with great opportunities for personal growth and self mastery. And yet as I stroll along city streets I am sad. Oh, the sight of the homeless is bad enough, however there is a much more pervasive sadness as I observe the masses of people walk by and those sitting inside the cafes.

I guess the best way to describe the feeling is a deep sense that as a culture we have lost the childlike connection with others and with the world around us. Technology in the form of cel phones, laptops and other devices seem to rule us. Please don't get me wrong. I think technology is great and am grateful to have access to it. However, I feel that there is a difference between it being our servant versus being our master.

Incessant tweeting, walking across the road staring at our phones, glued to our computers in just about every coffee shop in the city and even texting each other while on a date or when in the same room. Our communication for the most part comprises a whole bunch of sound bites, devoid of emotion, intuition and mostly, HEART. Where has healthy debate gone, emotional intimacy and appreciation for the magic of each moment. The world seems to be coming at us with greater and greater vengeance.

As I reflected on this reality before writing the book I came to an important realization. It was that the only thing different between my childhood days and the present is that the speed of technology has only exposed and exacerbated problems that have always existed. Fear, insecurity, depression and lack of self esteem have always influenced peoples lives, it's just that the degree and intensity of our awareness has multiplied a thousand fold. No wonder a recent study indicates that among millennials, over 54% say they plan to get off facebook, twitter and instagram. They sighted boredom and waste of time as some of the top reasons.

This only corroborates one of my strongest core beliefs which is that the rational mind, our analytical mind is a wonderful servant but a terrible master. **Our minds have truly gone wild**. I feel that as a society we have given much too much glory to our wily analytical mind. Formal education, creative thinking and gathering important knowledge is of course necessary, but hyperactive and negative thinking can be a killer.

If you're studying to be a doctor, lawyer or scientist then knowledge may well be power. But, when it comes to our day to day interpersonal relationships I would suggest that such things as compassion, patience, love, presence of mind and humor among other things have the most impact.

How many courses on these subjects did you have in school. No wonder the self help industry is a billion dollar industry.

As you read through the book you will notice that I make the importance of heart over mind a common theme as well as how our relationships with others are significantly impacted by the quality of the relationship we have with ourselves. We will see how the rational mind is only one piece of the whole inner engine, which also includes our human emotions, our physical bodies and the true guide I call our 'zen zone'. It is like the clear blue sky that is always the above the moving ever changing cloud formations. Unlike the hyperactive mind, it brings the inner peace, tranquility and joy most of us only have a glimpse of.

This book first and foremost is about my own personal journey in order to assure you that whatever wisdom I might have now comes from experiencing the very same issues you might be going through at this time. The rest of the book provides you with some of the practical solutions that can help fast track your transformation, based both on my own personal experience as well results of hundreds of clients who have participated in my 9 step program.

Growing up can be very challenging as we face many fears, anxieties and insecurities from such things as peer pressure from friends or expectations from family members. Unfortunately, very few of us experience true unconditional love early on in life which can explain how that armor around our little hearts can begin to develop early on in life; often necessary in order for us to survive.

Shutting down our hearts can lead to a turning inward in the form of timidity, shyness social anxiety which can then cause overreactions and a tendency to dominate, control or even bully others. These patterns can be very insidious and last a lifetime unless we choose at some point to take responsibility to heal our negative past and commit to taking charge of our own happiness and success in life.

I assume you have chosen to read this book because something is still holding you back from moving ahead in some area of your life. Many of us have invested much time and money in accumulating information, hiring a coach or attending highly charged motivational seminars and workshops. And so we are back for more? The truth is that most of us are looking for the next great idea, technique or experience that may just give us that extra edge in life both professionally and personally. If that is all you wish to achieve by reading this book, then you will likely find a few useful nuggets. Still many of you may be looking for a lot more than just a few good ideas.

Are you tired of 'dabbling' in personal growth; having been exposed to a variety of philosophies, concepts and techniques without seeing the results you truly desire? It may have been some form of visualization, meditation or communication workshop. You might have explored some form of therapy or learned how to do affirmations. I certainly have and benefitted from all of them. At times though it can be confusing and overwhelming, and rarely do we have access to a truly simple, comprehensive and practical approach to self-mastery that connects all the dots.

In my opinion our personal development journey needs to be less about how much knowledge we have accumulated and more about how we put our awareness into action and achieve real transformation. Reading books and attending motivational seminars alone are simply not enough. What we do with that knowledge and experience makes all the difference in the world. In the end, it's about mastering ourselves to a point where we no longer have to search for so many answers outside of ourselves. We can literally become our own life coach. That is why I have chosen to make this primarily a 'how to' book!

We live in a world that worships the rational mind and are inundated daily with thoughts, words and visual impressions. In my experience the rational mind has proven to be a good servant but a terrible master. And yet we are bombarded daily with a dose of thoughts and words exacerbated exponentially with social media. The question is at what cost? We may be more aware, more knowledgeable and more informed, but we are also more stressed out, more suspicious and more overwhelmed than ever. When is the last time you heard the word contentment?

Many of us have allowed our rational minds and imaginations to spin out of control, and that is why I take exception at times to the statement "knowledge is power". I believe that the heart is power, the human spirit is power, having a joyful spirit, presence of mind and patience are all power. The explosion of social media has left our experience of "hands on" interpersonal skills on the back burner.

The wise masters from the East who meditated in order to achieve enlightenment most often did so without reading a lot of books. They simply counted their breath from 1-10 to quiet their rational minds and go to a much deeper level of inner peace, clarity, wisdom and mental concentration. Do you want to get into top physical shape? If so, do you think about reading books or attending seminars? Likely not. You go to the gym for a physical fitness program.

Why then should it be any different for our approach to inner fitness? I will now introduce you to a different type of book; welcoming you to the inner gymnasium - the right place to get in top shape from the inside out. You will be able to access a method of getting the inner conditioning you need, the mental toughness you seek and the inner self confidence you desire in order to live a truly extraordinary life. You will learn how to ultimately "drop the armor" of your past and "unleash your inner warrior" to achieve ultimate success in life!

For the most part this book is designed to guide you through 9 successful solution steps. These steps will help you communicate with more clarity, confidence and impact from the inside out. If you practice these techniques consistently for 90 days, you will most certainly jump start your journey toward true inner fitness and communication mastery. I would like to make very clear that I am in no way criticizing other methods and approaches, as I have benefitted by many of them myself. I am simply saying if you are still stuck in some area of life, you might find these 9 steps to be a very powerful, complete and effective alternative.

Again, this is meant to be more of a how-to book, providing you with some valuable tips and practical tools you can use right now to improve your life. I could certainly have written a much more entertaining or philosophical book, but I felt a more practical one was the right and timely thing to do. I sensed that people today want something more than concepts; they desire something practical which they can implement and achieve in a relatively short period of time. That is why this book is less about reading and more about doing. When you work out at the gym, the experience can sometimes be repetitive and tedious, however when you look into the mirror after months of hard work, being pleased with the results is what really counts. Practicing what is taught here may seem a little like working out in the gym, but with persistence and determination you will find that your life begins to shape up in a way that you have always dreamed it would. You will discover how these 9 steps can help you attain your professional and personal goals more quickly and effectively. Many clients of mine who have gone through this program have consistently demonstrated significant results within ninety days.

The success rate can vary depending on an individual's background, commitment level or the strength of their desire to truly live in harmony with their life purpose. Many of you may choose to read the entire book in a short period of time. It is normal to want to access all the information as quickly as possible. For maximum results though, I recommend that you implement each step; one at a time, and really focus on that step until you feel you have mastered it. For some steps that may mean one day, and for others it may mean several weeks or even months.

So where are you in your life right now? You may feel discouraged from not achieving the success you desire in your career, relationships or in making an impact in the world. You may feel overwhelmed and stressed out, finding it a challenge to access those ever elusive feelings of contentment, happiness and pride in your achievements. Most of us share the same desire to live our lives to the fullest and hope that when it comes time to leave this world, we would all love to say we have no regrets. Sadly, many of us can't really say that and in fact for the most part, we are using a very small amount of our true personal potential. We may even feel that life is simply passing us by because we are not living out our true destiny and life purpose.

Well, in that regard you're definitely not alone and I can certainly relate from personal experience. Most humans today are not living anywhere close to their true potential, which may partly explain society's need for the billion dollar self-help industry. This industry—in the form of books, coaching and seminars—has already provided us with an abundance of information and insights about how to live our lives more successfully.

One reason that books and seminars might be so appealing is that there is always the hope for the quick fix for our day-to-day challenges in life. Ironically, we would never do that with our technological devices. I often ask my clients the following questions: "If your cell phone was working at only 30% of its efficiency, how quickly would you get it fixed? The same question applies with your laptop computer or your vehicle—would you settle for less than 100% efficiency or would you get them fixed right now?"

The universal answer is of course, "immediately". And yet when we get up in the morning and look into the mirror, are we similarly horrified at the fact that most of us are using a very small percentage of our personal potential? How many of us, with an intense sense of urgency, seek out ways to live fully that day? The sad reality is that most of us so readily accept mediocrity in ourselves and wonder why we are not achieving what we truly want out of life.

We live in a society that places so much attention on our physical well-being, often neglecting the importance of the condition of our inner world. The irony is that the inner, I believe, holds the key to success in all other areas of our lives, including our professional and personal relationships.

In fact, the success we aspire to in life greatly depends on how effectively we communicate with other people. Every day of our lives we are in communication with others, both personally and professionally. Aside from the actual words we speak, a huge part of our communication has to do with the intangibles. They include our level of passion and enthusiasm, patience, our ability to listen and to inspire. They include our level of self-confidence, assertiveness and our ability to think on our feet as we confront challenges with others.

Keep in mind that we are hanging out with ourselves 24/7, so we better be having a great relationship with numero uno. I know this might sound a little funny but if you think about it, we have been in an arranged marriage with ourselves from the moment we came out of the womb. Unfortunately, this most important relationship we have is the one we most often neglect. Why are we so damn hard on ourselves? We would never be so critical of our children, so why do *we* get the brunt of our own negativity? Do you wonder why there are so many dysfunctional relationships in our world today? I am convinced that most dysfunctional relationships are a direct result of the dysfunctional relationship we have with ourselves.

You may have read a lot of books, received university degrees and have all kinds of life and work experience, but if the castle is built on quicksand, sooner or later problems will begin to surface. That is why I ask each client who visits me for the first time the following question:

"WHAT'S HOLDING YOU BACK?"

What I usually tell them is that if they can fix the weak links in the relationship they have with themselves, then their relationships with others will flow much more effortlessly.

So that is my question to you right now: What is holding YOU back?

Is it procrastination, fear, lack of vision, insecurity, jealousy or lack of motivation? Perhaps poor leadership skills, low self-confidence, lack of time management skills or a scattered mind? Are you anxious, worried, impatient, or simply needing to master your communication skills?

These are only some of the things that may be keeping you from living a more fulfilling and successful life. At the end of the day, most of us are looking for the same things. We want to have success at work. We want fulfilling relationships and generally to feel happy and content in life. It is easier said than done. In order to achieve all of this requires effective communication skills in both our professional and personal lives. But again I emphasize that those skills depend for the most part on the quality of the relationship we have with ourselves.

Before moving on, it may be valuable for me to share some insights into my personal background. You may then understand that this program was not merely created from ideas and concepts alone, but rather mostly from my own life experiences and relationships with a wide variety of people. As you read about my experience, please remember that your own journey is unique to you. It is not about comparing our life experiences, but more about learning how some of the insights and solutions may apply to each of our journeys. It is also important to be grateful for all that we experience from life because however challenging it may seem at times, each step builds on the next, depending of course on whether we choose to learn from our experiences or not.

Who you are at this very moment is a result of all your accumulated learning. As you read about my journey, you may wish to reflect on your own, and however positive or negative the memories may be, try to acknowledge the significant role your past has played in your life. It is not about how difficult or unpleasant some of it may have been, it is more about what you have done about it, and more importantly what you will do now to take your life to a whole new level. In fact, with the help of the 9-step program, you can now speed along much quicker than I was able to.

My Personal Story

My older brother Larry was a tough act to follow. He graduated at the top of his class from medical school, he was a great athlete and was crowned King of his high school because of his popularity. If that was not enough, he was nicknamed "Dean" by some of his friends because he looked so much like the very handsome Rat Pack crooner, Dean Martin.

As for me, aside from being a pretty good athlete, I was a very average student, quite insecure around girls, and felt the brunt of repeatedly being compared to my brother. So I learned early on that life would not be a cakewalk. Like all of us I would have to face fears, worries and insecurities, and discover that these challenges were all part of the curriculum of being human. I later learned that with the right mindset, these obstacles could in fact become opportunities for me to grow, stretch and turn life's lemons into lemonade.

My first big life-changing experience came at the age of 19 when I gave a speech in front of a large crowd being the best man at my brother's wedding. Keep in mind that as a teenager, I was "a jock" who found it quite challenging to communicate articulately and coherently one to one, let alone in front of large audiences. I can so vividly remember how nervous I was as I began to speak to over three hundred people. Although I must admit it did help that I consumed a few screw drivers before the talk.

At the end of the speech, I was totally taken by surprise as people flocked up to me expressing congratulations with great adulation. Some were even encouraging me to pursue being a professional best man for other people's weddings. The crowd seemed to be touched by my message and in my ability to communicate with such clarity, confidence and impact. I felt pleasantly surprised by their kind words and acknowledgments, but at the same time I found it quite confusing. On one hand I had just experienced a temporary glimpse into my potential as a speaker and communicator, but on the other hand I had no idea what all this meant, nor what I could do to act on it.

I truly feel that the experience planted a seed in me that would eventually germinate, becoming a major motivator in my pursuit toward a career in public speaking. I knew I had a gift and some talent, but little did I know how long it would take for them to truly blossom. I spent the next few years in limbo feeling somewhat lost and lacking in purpose. Like so many others who suffer from self-doubt, I became a professional procrastinator. It actually took another life-changing experience to shake me out of the doldrums.

LIFE-CHANGING EXPERIENCE

Following the death of my father, I decided to take a year off from university. My goal was to spread my wings and travel around the world in order to gain further life experience. Six months later I came face to face with my own mortality; coming within a whisker of dying from a heat stroke near the Mediterranean Sea. I had spent the day alone by the water in 120 degree Fahrenheit weather. I walked about ten miles to get there with no hat and only a tomato and piece of bread to eat. Certainly not the smartest idea in the world. As I began the long treck back along the desert at the end of the day with no one in sight I noticed that my heart began beating very rapidly. I was completely alone and realized that something was very wrong. An inner panic began to set in and a terrible feeling of doom surrounded me I resigned to the thought that I was about to die.

I finally past out thinking my time had truly come. To my extreme astonishment, the next thing I knew I was awake on the balcony of a farming family, whom I later discovered miraculously found me and transported me to their home miles away. To this day, I'm not quite sure how they found me, but they did say I had severe heat stroke—a common cause of death for many soldiers in that part of the world.

After such a terrifying experience, I became conscious of how afraid of death I was, something I had never thought about before. For the first time in my life I became open to exploring the spiritual side of my life and made a conscious decision to truly connect with myself on a much deeper level. I wanted to know if there was more to life than the physical reality of the world around me because until that time I was quite resistant to anything religious or spiritual.

It is truly fascinating how the experience of coming so close to death can shake you to your core, get you out of your mind, humble you and give you a feeling of openness to a much deeper level of being. I guess I was truly ready for a spiritual awakening; however, because of my skepticism

I insisted that it would need to be real and from actual experience, not just blind belief.

So I returned home knowing down deep that my life would never be the same. No matter how much I immersed myself into my career and into relationships, something deep down seemed to be missing; an underlying empty feeling that was undeniable. It was as if my soul was crying out to be heard and experienced. Then one day, while browsing in a local bookstore, I met a charming lady who struck up a conversation with me about spirituality.

I was especially impressed by the depth I observed in her eyes and the clarity that resonated from her voice. She projected a genuine calmness and loving spirit that I felt instantaneously. I am not speaking here of romantic love, but rather a much deeper kind of love in the form of compassion, inner peace and joy. I knew right there and then that she had something that I wanted.

She introduced me to a local meditation center she was a member of, which later became a monastery and convent. Everyone I met there seemed to have a similar quality of depth, contentment and compassion. The experience was so compelling for me that within a week I moved in, and thus began an interesting stage of my life, living as a monk for over nine years.

These 9 years were an incredible experience. I look back at them with fondness despite being ridiculed by friends for wasting all those prime years of my life. The reality is that no matter what I ended up sacrificing in my outside lifestyle, I created the most solid foundation for the next part of my journey when I returned to the real world. Yes, we lived mostly in silence, minimal chit chat, which I loved, meditated 4 times a day and did various forms of physical labor to survive. Quite often we would sleep on the floor with a thin mat, and I will never forgot the bell that woke us up at 3:30 am ready to get in our first 2 hours of meditation that day.

We all contributed in making the meals, pretty basic stuff including rice, vegetables, bread, soup and how I loved my peanut butter sandwiches. The highlight of course was when we baked our greatest delicacy we called 'hockey puck muffins'. The focal point of that life was the meditation practice where we all strived to become enlightened as tapping into and staying in the **zen zone** was the end game.

With the help of wonderful mentors, I was able to access considerable levels of inner peace, contentment and joy that I never knew possible. However grateful I was for the experience, after nine years of the ascetic lifestyle, I became restless. I began to see that meditation and accessing the zen however important would never be enough. I knew intuitively that I would have to connect it with day to day life. My heart longed to get the full experience of North American lifestyle.

I knew that if I was to truly grow into a more complete person, it would have to be beyond the comfort of being so isolated from society at large. I understood that if my spiritual experience was worth its salt, I would have to integrate what I had learned as a monk into a "real life" North American context. Oh, did I mention that I also missed the company of women and other things that the western culture offered? It was clear that if I was to continue on in the inner zen zone work I would have to integrate this practice into every area of my life, including career, relationships and community involvement.

I was more excited and committed than ever to grow as a person in every way that I could. I felt strongly that if I was to truly have a positive impact on others, I better become a true master and not just a teacher. I wanted to use all of my talents and skills to make a difference in the world. I had a feel for public speaking, coaching and training, remembering that over the years, friends and acquaintances often felt at ease asking for my advice. Although I was pretty good at giving advice, I knew that I had so much more growing to do if I was to truly have a genuine impact on others. I would have to walk the talk. I learned early on that there is a big difference between being a teacher and a master. There are many teachers, but few masters.

Our Addiction to Knowledge

I have always questioned the relevance and quality of some aspects of the North American educational system. I am not referring here to the quality of teachers or the curriculums taught. Rather, I question how effectively we are teaching students human skills, communication and personal development skills; all so critical for their success in life after school.

Our traditional educational system seems to overly focus on rational and analytical learning; centering much more on knowledge and much less on experiential learning. We seem to disproportionately honor technology, science, mathematics and other areas that exercise and expand our rational minds. But what about the more right brain functions like our life purpose, humor, creativity, intuition, entrepreneurship and general communication skills; all so relevant for mastering many areas of our lives.

No doubt left brain learning is highly important not only for our mental development but also for how we can use important knowledge to impact the world. However, if it is not balanced with right brain learning we not only deprive our children of a truly well balanced education but also open up Pandora's Box of social ills. Look at the social problems that plague the world today, and we can more clearly see how many of them have to do with some form of mental sickness or communication breakdown. Depression, bullying, ADD, jealousy, feelings of insecurity, divorce rates, social as well sexual abuse and hunger for power and control; most of these have everything to do with the breakdown in our relationships with others and the relationship we have with ourselves. Yes we are certainly paying the price for holding on to an archaic school system.

News we are fed daily most often feature stories about war, shootings, bullying, domestic violence, racism and the like. Although on the surface they all become social issues, if we look into the deeper causes often it can be traced back to the individual's feelings of fear, anxiety, depression, helplessness, insecurity and lack of self worth. We all face injustices in our lives and hopefully we work together to correct them, but the one thing we can always change is how we think, feel and act.

The real question is how do we respond to these challenges, do we become the victim of them and continually blame others, or do we choose to empower ourselves and contribute positive change in the world around us. Can you imagine how different our world would be if our school system focused as much on communication and life skills as they do on mathematics, biology and chemistry?

When students graduate from University, most of what they will face in life has much more to do with relationships and communication than it does applying practical knowledge they have spent years learning. Wisdom, compassion and self-confidence often go further in life than getting good grades, and yet very little of that is taught in our traditional school systems.

For example, doctors who are compassionate, understanding and socially savvy have much more impact in providing a trusting doctor-patient relationship than those who do not demonstrate these qualities. Please don't get me wrong, knowledge is very important and should always be encouraged. I am simply saying that unless it is balanced with learning interpersonal and personal development skills, success will be limited.

However important getting good grades are, what may be just as important is how clear, motivated and confident you are about taking charge of your life when enter the "real world". These qualities are less tangible and often ignored in our very "knowledge focused" school systems. That is why there are countless examples of successful entrepreneurs who have actually had very little formal education. I know many myself and I can tell you first hand that most if not all have great attitudes, work ethic and people skills.

True personal growth should often begin with clearing the mind and accessing the intuitive mind which in fact is a much more dependable resource to run our life ship. If we tap into what psychologists call the alpha state more consistently, we will likely find that the intuitive mind will be an effective leader for our rational mind, as well as for our emotions and physical body. If we allow our mind or emotions to run us, all hell will certainly break loose sooner or later. But with the zen zone leading, inner peace, focus, and true success will certainly follow.

Now that you have a better idea about my background and some of my philosophies related to self improvement and personal growth, I will let you in on another reason I chose to write this book. The theme of accepting, loving and respecting yourself as a foundation for having great relationships does not just come out of a vacuum, nor from reading books. In part it comes from my own personal experiences but also from 25 years of observation within my own personal coaching practice. To help back up this notion I thought it might be valuable to share about a dozen of the most common questions I get asked by clients. If you study the answers you will see almost every one of them goes back to the importance of the relationship we have with ourselves.

COACH'S CORNER

I have been coaching and training for over 25 years working with thousands of people with diverse backgrounds and personalities. The interesting thing I repeatedly observe is that despite the obvious cultural differences, we all in fact share many of the same personal issues, experiences and life challenges. To drive this point home I thought this might be a good time to answer some of the common questions I get asked in order to demonstrate the importance of personal development being such an important foundation in all of our relationships.

PROCRASTINATION

Q.   *I have a pattern of putting things off and sometimes I feel like life is passing me by. How can I overcome that feeling?*

A.   Procrastination is all about choosing not to take action when we know that action is appropriate and important, most often due to some underlying psychological or emotional block. Our thoughts are connected to our emotions which in turn are connected to our actions, which are ultimately connected to our communication with others. If our thoughts are positive and clear and our emotions are full of passion, enthusiasm and belief in ourselves then a natural result will be that our actions usually follow quite easily and naturally. However, if our thoughts and emotions are somewhat turbulent in the form of negative thinking, fear, worry or insecurity, our decisions to take effective action will likely be compromised.

To solve this, the first step is to become aware and acknowledge the pattern. The second step is to get fed up with being that way. The third is to commit 100% to changing the behavior now! Whether it's speaking in front of a group, avoiding getting the dishes done, pursuing your dream career, studying for exams or attracting desired relationships, you can turn procrastination into action easier than you think. When you master steps 3-7 later in the book, you will likely never procrastinate again.

30 SECOND ELEVATOR SPEECH

Q.   *I am in sales and know how important the 30 second elevator speech is, and yet I really struggle with it. Do you have any advice?*

A.   I am of the opinion that the 30 second elevator speech is quite over rated. We often struggle to find those perfect set of words that will magically draw potential clients our way. The truth is, what is most important when first connecting with someone is to build trust, confidence and likeability. It is much more important for us to be genuine, personable and kind rather than opportunistically trying to sell something too quickly.

Being overly eager to impress is a mistake that many salespeople and entrepreneurs make. The irony is that if we can simply enjoy connecting in a genuine and very human way with people, we would more likely find that our business soars to a whole new level. Quality rapport building is by far your most effective 30 second elevator speech. That said, there is still room for you to respond when someone asks you the question "what do you do?" Just make sure your response focuses less on what you do and more on how you help people. A less aggressive approach normally produces greater results.

THE PAIN OF UNRECIPROCATED LOVE

Q. *I have had some very painful breakups and mostly they are about me being rejected by someone who I love more than they love me. Any advice?*

A. Unreciprocated love is one of the most painful of all life experiences, and I know about that pattern first hand. There are two ways you can respond to that kind of pain. The first is to become the victim of the pain, shut down and potentially experience an endless round of dysfunctional relationships. Or, you can use the painful experience to grow as a person and enter into future relationships with this learned understanding. If you choose to be the victim of the pain, you then risk building a protective wall around your heart, vowing never to be hurt again. This could lead to a build up of anger, fear and sadness; causing you to indulge in negative attitudes toward relationships and love.

The best choice is to learn from your pain. Being rejected by someone simply triggers in us our own fears and insecurities about ourselves. It actually takes a lot of courage to acknowledge the pain, express it constructively and then release it. The next step is to analyze what the best qualities of the relationship were; what we actually liked and disliked about it. When we are obsessed with someone we tend to only look at the qualities we strongly admire in them and overlook the flaws. We may assume that the flaws will just go away, or that in time we will change them. Good luck with that!

Having the courage to face the breakup and move on allows us to consider in a more logical way why we were so attracted to such a relationship in the first place and how we can avoid that same pattern going forward. Until our next relationship we can choose to focus on the following. First, to build ourselves up mentally, physically and professionally; thereby projecting a vibe that is much more conducive to attracting more loving and quality relationships. Second, we can become more effective at assessing and evaluating the next person we begin to date. Slowing down during the courtship process generally ensures greater awareness of the true quality of the relationship.

MANAGING STRESS

Q. *There is way too much stress in my life, how can I manage it more effectively?*

A. There are many types of stress. To name a few, stress can be about money, health or relationships. When we become aware of stress in our lives the first thing to do is to identify "why"? There are times when the source of our stress is outside ourselves and the solution is found in the environment around us. There are times for example that changing where we live can decrease the stress. This may relate to convenience, the quality of community around us or other environmental factors. Sometimes it has to do with relational stress that requires either healing the relationship or ending it.

I have found that the vast majority of our stress comes from how we ourselves manage external stress. There are many times when external changes are not possible, and the only way for us to manage our stress comes from our own commitment to changing attitudes and our commitment to self mastery. Once you become aware of the true source of the stress you can then more easily focus on finding the most effective solution to it.

IS THERE SUCH A THING AS SOULMATES

Q. *I have trouble accepting that soulmates exist. I want to believe it but I am skeptical. Your thoughts?*

A.   If you mean by soulmates, relationships that are connected on many levels including physical, emotional, lifestyle and soul connection, yes I know them to be true from my own experience and in others I have observed. However, in my opinion, being with a soulmate is not the most important thing. I feel it is more important be in a relationship that is right for you. There are many types of relationships.

Some are co-dependant or dysfunctional, some are great friends offering areas of compatibility but with no deep connection, and still others are of a high level soul mate quality relationship which borders on being magical. Whatever type of relationship you are in, what is most essential is that both of you are willing to work on yourselves and the relationship. A big part of that initially is about building trust, confidence and enjoying great communication together. For those of you that strongly desire to be in a soul mate level relationship, the key is to activate your own inner soul mate by first learning to accept, love and respect yourself, like you would your own child. In the first 7 of the 9 steps are all about empowering yourself, it's all about creating the foundation you need, not only to attract a high quality relationship but also be able to sustain it long term.

FEAR OF PUBLIC SPEAKING

Q. *I am terrified when speaking in front of large groups, how can I overcome my fear?*

A. There are two common reasons why so many of us fear public speaking. The first is we are not clear or competent about what we plan to talk about. The obvious solution is to have some sort of structure to our talk and to have enough knowledge about the subject in order to present ourselves as somewhat of an expert in the field. The second reason for our anxiety around public speaking is our fear of being judged or ridiculed. To compensate, many of us become perfectionists, trying too hard to be "perfect". The fact is, the opposite is true. It is more important to be genuine and authentic than it is to try to be "perfect".

To help understand the importance of this, I can tell you that I consider the old Rat Packer Dean Martin to have been one of the greatest personalities and entertainers ever. In the 1960's NBC wanted him to do a variety show and he said "no" many times because he valued his lifestyle and did not want to commit to rehearsing all week. They finally agreed to give him a show on the condition that he show up a few hours before the show, while others slaved in rehearsals all week.

He mostly improvised, made mistakes and people loved him. In fact over 50,000,000 people watched him weekly from around the world on a variety show that was #1 for almost a decade. If you YouTube "Dean Martin", Florence Henderson (from the Brady Bunch) did a five minute interview honoring what Dean Martin taught her about spontaneity and authenticity. I do not mean in anyway that being prepared and knowledgeable on a particular subject is not important, rather, I am equally stressing the importance of spontaneity, authenticity and likeability.

As you learn more about the 9 steps later in this book, with special focus on step #4 "Unleash Your Inner Warrior", you will learn how to master some of these fears and insecurities and learn how you can get up in front of any group at any time and be a genuine and effective presenter.

HYPERACTIVE MIND

Q. *My mind is always going and never stops. I am not sure I know what true inner peace is. How do I quiet my mind?*

A. Rest assured that the mind can be quieted. The first step is to identify why specifically it is so hyperactive. An ongoing hyperactive mind is usually a sign of "the mind gone wild", and may be a sign of not enough relaxation or down time, so taking more vacations or doing spiritual exercises such as yoga or meditation can be very beneficial. Other times it has more to do with emotional and psychological issues. For example, if you had some challenges in your relationships and have a pattern of getting your heart broken.

A common response by most would be to create a big wall around our hearts, imagining that will protect us from further pain and hurt. Shutting down our feelings usually means that we likely overcompensate by putting too much attention on our rational mind, often resulting in hyperactive and negative thinking. In other cases we may obsess our physical bodies. Sometimes we delude ourselves when we try to protect our heart because we think we are avoiding pain. But in truth we are just over stimulating the mind or body and by doing so we open ourselves up to burn out and feelings of anxiety; the very thing we are trying to protect ourselves from in the first place. We make the mistake of assuming that we can suppress our emotions without experiencing the consequences. When we feel emotional pain we either shut down, over react or take the middle path of acknowledging the pain, expressing it constructively and then taking responsibility to grow from our experience. The point is that if we balance our body, mind and emotions in a healthy way, we will more likely solve the issue of having a hyperactive mind.

CAN'T SAY NO

Q. *I guess you would call me the ultimate people pleaser, as I have a lot of trouble saying "no". The result is that people take advantage of my good nature. How do I overcome this habit?*

A. Most often this pattern is rooted in lack of self respect. As children, most of us craved love and respect that we may have never actually received. This stage of life is so critical to our later growth and maturity that we may spend decades or an entire lifetime working very hard to be liked by others. It's one thing to enjoy being liked and quite another thing to be desperately needing to be liked. In the latter case it can become an obsession for many of us who will literally do anything to earn respect from others.

We do this by being overly nice to people in order to avoid rejection or confrontation. Quite often it means we just can't say "no". We can become so pre-occupied with what others think about us, we abandon healthy personal boundaries by disproportionately bending over backwards in order to please. That strategy often backfires. The more we try to please, the more others will either take advantage of us or end up disrespecting us because they feed on our fears and insecurities which are behind it all. The solution to this dilemma is to become aware of how fed up we are with this pattern and strongly commit to let it go. First and foremost we need to respect ourselves before we genuinely and effectively can impact others and earn their respect. By learning this important life lesson, there will no longer be such a need to obsessively seek approval from others.

THE STATE OF THE WORLD IS GETTING ME DOWN

Q. *There is so much negative news today what with wars, global warming, financial stress and so on. How do I remain positive within this chaos?*

A. It is quite true that most of us are no longer living simple lives as the world has become such a complex place to live in, especially with the rapid and ever changing growth of technology. I am sure that stress has always been part of the human condition, but never have we been as bombarded by so many outside forces as we are today. The key words here are "outside forces" because it is important to realize that there are both internal stress factors as well as external ones. There is only so much we can do to control the outside forces. Oh sure, we can change some of the external stressors like letting go of negative influences, changing jobs or by managing our day to day schedules.

However, in most cases we do not have direct control over changing anything. There is not much we can do when a sunny day turns to rain or we lose our jobs or someone close to us suddenly passes away. These events certainly make us feel sad, fearful or depressed, but the good news is that we don't have to stay in this state of mind. Hopefully we come to realize that the only thing we truly control moment to moment are our own attitudes. We can choose how we think, feel, act and communicate toward others. We have the power to create our own good news despite the circumstances around us. It is all about our response to each moment. If we live our lives less as victims of circumstance and more as someone who is taking charge of what we *can* control, we will more likely live a very fulfilling life and have a positive impact on many along the way.

I AM NOT ATTRACTED TO THOSE WHO ARE ATTRACTED TO ME

Q. *Why is that I am not attracted to the ones who are attracted to me, and the ones I am attracted to are generally not attracted to me?*

A. After years of coaching and through my own personal experiences, I am quite convinced that when it comes to love most of us are looking for mommy or daddy in a younger body. As I said earlier, most of us did not receive the love and respect we craved for early on in life. There is no blame here as our parents did the best they could. So from a very early age we conditioned ourselves to think that we were not worthy of love.

As we grew into our teens and beyond, these deep rooted beliefs remain with us consciously or unconsciously. And yet, when it comes to the affairs of the heart we remain committed to finding that true love. Even the language of "they broke my heart", "I want to find the love of my life" or "it's so hard to get the love I want" is all about "what I want and need" as opposed to the love I want to share with someone who is deserving of my love.

Until we give ourselves the very love and respect that we are looking for from someone else, we will never overcome that pain of not getting the love we want. If instead of looking outside of ourselves, we actually took the time to heal our past issues and commit to our personal growth as a healthy and well balanced person, we would not be as *needy* looking for love. Rather, our focus would be about sharing the love we already have within us, with another person who can love us back equally.

You can now see by these questions and answers the important role our inner world plays in our day to day challenges of life. You now have a better idea of my background, philosophy and some of the common themes I have addressed as a coach and trainer. You also have an idea of my use of the phrase "Inner Fitness" making the point that it is time we take the personal development world from a focus of awareness to action and result. It's time to get into the inner gym and build those inner muscles we all need in order to live a life full of joy, love and success.

Having spent many years as a coach and trainer I began to observe some very common issues that were holding my clients back in their business and personal lives. I also intuitively knew that counseling and mentoring them, however helpful, would not be enough. I felt the need to create a program which would out live my coaching and provide each client with a practical system and roadmap so they would literally become their own coach.

The 9 Step Formula

I mentioned at the beginning that this is mainly a "how to" book. Now that you have a context for how I came to develop the program through my own personal educational and coaching experiences, the rest of this book will focus primarily on the 9 steps. When it comes to self-development, often our learning takes place in bits and pieces and with a "hit or miss" approach. At some point we may learn a form of meditation or a therapeutic way to heal from past pain experiences.

Other times we may learn to do a form of affirmations or positive thinking exercises. Each process may be very valuable, but often lacks connectedness to a truly integrated approach that can make our personal development journey more complete, rapid and effective. That is what the program is all about. The following is a brief description of each part:

Step 1: **Connect with your Present** is about having the courage to look into the mirror and assess the strengths and weaknesses you see.

Step 2: **Connect with your Past** is about neutralizing the self-limiting beliefs and patterns from your past, that keep you from successfully moving ahead

Step 3: Connect with your Vision is about clarifying what you want out of life and discovering a larger purpose.

Step 4: Connect with your Inner Power is about strengthening mental toughness, determination and overall inner self-confidence.

Step 5: Connect with your Actions is about all about achieving success through action both professionally and personally.

Step 6: Connect with your Challenges is about maintaining presence of mind and equanimity while experiencing the obstacles and challenges of life.

Step 7: Connect with your Magnetism is about enjoying an incredible state of grace, inner freedom and synchronicity.

Step 8: Connect with Others is about perfecting the art of communication both professionally and personally.

Step 9: Connect with the World is about creating master mind groups for the purpose of making a difference in the world.

MIND
GONE
WILD

PART 2

Step #1 Connect With Your Present

"Only when the clamor of the outside world is silenced will you be able to hear the deeper vibration. Listen carefully."

—*Sarah Ban Breathnach*

Suppose you decide to get into top physical shape and are very committed to do whatever it takes to achieve this goal. One option you have is to hire a fitness trainer, and the first thing they will do is to assess your current physical condition. It takes courage to admit that you need help, acknowledge your current physical state and set out toward achieving the fitness goals you set for yourself. It works the very same way when it comes to your level of inner fitness.

Before we begin the journey of activating our inner power, it is essential to observe and evaluate the state of our current life condition. It is important to identify the areas of strength and weakness in our lives so we can create an effective plan of action. That might sound logical and obvious to most of you, but I can tell you that many people never achieve what they truly want, partly because they are not willing to take the important first step of self reflection and assessment. It takes some humility and courage to look in the mirror and make the adjustments necessary to live your life in a well balanced way. Some of us are really good at distracting ourselves with busyness as a way to avoid looking inside. Some obsess on politics, some on making money and still others on a personal relationship.

In today's world, there is certainly an abundance of outside distractions and influences for us to choose from: cell phones, text messaging, e-mails, blogs, news feeds; not to mention our family responsibilities. It becomes easy for us to put the most important relationship we have on the back burner, the relationship we have with ourselves. In fact, the quality of every other relationship we have, be it personal or professional, depends on the energy, passion and confidence we have within ourselves, so it really is best to give it the attention it needs. Just the fact that you are open to reading this book shows that you are willing to take that first step, and I commend you for that.

If you procrastinate, you are then depriving yourself and others from experiencing *you* at your very best. If you are overly insecure you are more likely to attract co-dependent and toxic relationships. If you are stressed out, that anxiety will be felt and noticed by others, whether they tell you or not, depriving them of a calm, content and centered *you*. These inner dysfunctions will ooze out of you whether you like it or not, and will adversely affect every one of your day to day relationships with others. That is why it is essential, as a first step in the journey of personal development to STOP, LOOK and LISTEN, and *take stock of your life.*

Obstacles and Challenges

It is easy to feel that our personal struggles in life are unique and limited to ourselves alone. Of course that notion is inaccurate. The truth is that most human beings share so many of the same obstacles and challenges. Let's explore some of the common challenges we all experience in day to day life:

PROCRASTINATION

I am always amazed at how many people readily admit to being chronic procrastinators. Not taking action in areas that would only enhance their lives makes no logical sense. So the question is "why is this condition so pandemic"? There are a number of explanations, I'm sure. One reason could be due to a person's lack of confidence. Say, for example, your dream is to be a famous singer. The very thought evokes much passion in you, but then the rational mind in the form of self-doubt kicks in where you may allow the self-limiting beliefs and emotions to sabotage that exciting dream.

Last year while visiting a friend in a palliative care unit, I spent time speaking with some of the patients, and I can tell you that not one person said they wish they would have spent more time in the office. An example of some of their responses include: *"I wish I had more fulfilling relationships"* and "I *wish I had pursued my true passion in the area of writing."* So procrastination is simply the result of self-defeating attitudes and beliefs that stifle our commitment to take action toward fulfilling our lives and achieving success.

FEAR OF REJECTION

The reasons we procrastinate are often rooted in fear and toxic thinking. Fear itself is not really the problem, as it is only when we become victims of that fear that it begins to be a real issue. Being nervous on our first date is normal, but does not necessarily keep us from going out and having a fabulous time. However, if we allow that initial nervousness to spiral out of control, to the point that we cancel the date, we have then become the victim of that fear. Love is good, obsession is a problem. Caution may be a good thing, phobia is not. Sadness is human, but depression ruins our lives. The truth is that we should be the master of our thoughts and emotions, not the other way around.

When someone is victimized by fear of rejection, it usually means they had some form of traumatic experience in their past which continues to permeate their consciousness in the present and limits their ability to take effective action.

As the mind and emotions begin to spin out of control, the inner engine begins to break down, and of course, negatively influences our day to day actions and communications with other people. It may show up in our body language and certainly in our voices and overall energy. If you fear rejection from others, it usually means that you have already rejected yourself. Being timid and shy is one form of fear of rejection, and ironically, so is bullying and acting overly aggressively. Both are rooted in insecurity, just on the opposite side of the same coin. If on the other hand, you have a healthy sense of self, you would not be adversely affected by rejection or criticism from others. You would know in your heart that although others may reject you, YOU DO NOT REJECT YOURSELF.

ANGER

There are healthy forms of anger and unhealthy ones. Healthy anger could take the form of you being upset at yourself for your tendency to procrastinate, but then you finally get fed up and begin to take action. That's a good use of anger. Unhealthy anger relates more to when you dwell on the resentful feelings and focus more on blaming yourself or others, rather than finding the appropriate solution to those disproportionate feelings.

Most people who remain angry usually have all the justifications in the world for their anger and will likely talk your ear off trying to convince you why their harbored feelings are so justified. They generally are more committed to being RIGHT than they are to being FREE. In the end, we can either allow ourselves to become the victim of our anger or take responsibility for channeling the anger into constructive solutions.

FEAR OF FAILURE

Fear of failure is often rooted in early life pressures placed on us by parents, teachers or friends. If for example, you had parents who were perfectionists and controlling and were more interested in you becoming who they wanted you to be, rather than supporting you in who *you* wanted to be, that's pressure. As a young child we are so dependent on others for our survival. We need love and support, and in the case of our parents, the child will likely do whatever it takes to please them. Do you now have a better idea of why so few people are pursuing their life passion? The reality for most of us is that by the time we become a teenager, we have accumulated more than our share of emotional and psychological baggage which can certainly get in the way of fearlessly pursuing our dreams. No wonder why the self help world today is such a huge industry!

SADNESS AND DEPRESSION

As you welll know, many of us today live high stress fast-paced lifestyles. As a result many have turned to recreational drugs and alcohol as a way to cope or escape from that stress. There is always the latest "wonder medication" for just about anything that ails us physically or emotionally, including depression. Depression is no more than a buildup of feelings of sadness.

Much of the media hype about medication is to convince us that the answer to our pain is to get a "quick fix" solution by addressing the symptom. Although medications at specific times may be very helpful to take the edge off our pain and provide some time to heal, in most cases they seem to be used as a crutch. They end up being used as a way to avoid looking in the mirror with courage, conviction and a true sense of self-responsibility.

The point of this chapter is not to create a shopping list of our problems. It is more about having the honesty to observe our current life condition so that we can once and for all solve whatever needs to be solved, and begin the process of living our lives more contentedly and successfully.

This then would be a good time for you to take a self-assessment and evaluation to view your current life condition. This is not a test or an exam. It's simply meant to give you an overview of your strengths and weaknesses and better enable you to prioritize your goals later in step #5, which is all about *Taking Charge of your Life*. I recommend that you take this assessment every month or two to observe the improvements in your scores.

It will help you chart your progress and allows you to acknowledge yourself for the advances you are making.

I recommend you rate yourself on a scale from 1-100% in the following categories. Your rating is based on how you feel about yourself in each category over the last few months in general, not because you had a bad day yesterday:

___ Physical Fitness	___ Listening Skills
___ Financial Health	___ Fun and Leisure
___ Patience	___ Networking Skills
___ Self Confidence	___ Leadership Skills
___ Time Management	___ Emotional Health
___ Vision	___ Marketing Strategies
___ Assertiveness	___ Productivity
___ Career Satisfaction	___ Public Speaking
___ Inner Peace	___ Relationships
___ Verbal Communication	___ Spirituality

Now you have a better idea of what your strengths and weaknesses are and an idea of what needs to be worked on in order to better yourself in every area of your life. Congratulations for completing the first step of the 9 steps.

Connect with Your Present - Overview

In this chapter, we encouraged you to re-assess your current life condition. It included a self-assessment and evaluation exercise designed to help you to clarify where you are at this time in your life, both professionally and personally.

Once completed, you will be ready for the section called "Connect with your Past"

The following are common questions we receive about Connect with your Present:

Q. ***The numbers I scored myself with would be very different than how others would see me. Are they really accurate then?***

A. They are accurate because the point of this exercise is to merely get a feel of how you would rate yourself. For the purpose of this exercise, it is not really important to know what others think of you, or even what you think you should be. It is more about how *you* feel about yourself in these areas right now.

Q. *My numbers are constantly in a state of change, how can I really gauge the true accuracy of the numbers?*

A. That is why we recommend that you give yourself an *average* of how you feel over the last two or three months in general. Keep in mind we are not doing a detailed accounting here. We simply want to get a general x-ray of your current lifestyle condition so you can then see what areas you most need to focus on in order to get to the next level of happiness and success.

Q. *I found myself to be quite discouraged when I looked at my scores and started to beat myself up, feeling like a "loser". How would you respond to that?*

A. Doing this exercise is a first step in the personal success journey and it requires courage and honesty to do it. Each person will have different feelings and reactions while doing it, depending on how they score themselves. Feeling down about your scores is not a bad thing because it really depends on what you *do* with those feelings. Obviously, if you indulge in them, then you risk descending into self-pity and self-flagellation, which won't serve any useful purpose. If, on the other hand, you channel your negative feelings into a commitment and strong resolve to turn things around, that would be a positive way to deal with the emotions. It's all about what you *do* with your feelings. Being fed up with mediocrity is a good thing if it mobilizes you into taking action!

Q. *What you say makes a lot of sense and sometimes I try to get my husband to look in the mirror, but he refuses to do that. What can I do?*

A. Taking stock of your own life does not mean imposing it on anyone else. If your husband is not open to growing, you cannot force him to do that. All you can do is focus on the one person you can control and that is YOU! Some people will be inspired by your example and want to do the same, while others will feel somewhat threatened by it or simply not be interested. You cannot help anyone to grow who does not want to.

Step #2 Connect With Your Past

"By letting it go it all gets done. The world is won by those who let it go. But when you try and try. The world is beyond the winning."

—*Lao Tzu*

Now that you have a clearer idea about what your strengths and weaknesses are, you are ready to address the root cause of what continues to hold you back. We have to remember that we come into this world with a pretty clean slate; like a new computer you may have just purchased. Over time however, viruses may get inside and keep it from functioning at the highest level of efficiency. In the very same way we sometimes allow inner viruses to accumulate in the form of negative thoughts and feelings.

We then have a choice to either become victims of these thoughts or feelings or use them as opportunities for growth. Some of the more negative thoughts and feelings may remain with us for a long time, lying dormant within us like some form of "inner parasite". Similar to doing a nutritional cleanse, we can choose to do a type of 'inner fitness cleanse'. Before we can effectively move on toward higher levels of personal growth, we first need to clear out the negativity of the past to make room for the positive elements we will allow in, during the later steps.

Most of us realize that our baggage from the past, in some small or large way, continues to limit our growth in the present and future. Many are of the opinion that we should just let go of the past and get on with our lives. That is easier said than done. The problem with this simplistic method of positive thinking is that it often provides no more than a band-aid effect, covering up emotions that need to be met head on before they can be released. The infection needs to *come out* of the body before true healing and growth takes place. That is why in many cases we cannot bypass step #2 in this step by step process.

Let's say, for example, that you have some negative past experience around a personal relationship. In your mind, you may believe that the painful experience is a thing of the past and that it has very little effect on you in the present. You're convinced that since you have grown so much as a person and the events took place so long ago that you are beyond it ever bothering you again.

Then out of the blue, you meet someone who turns your life upside down. All of a sudden, that individuals mere presence in your life sets off deep-rooted and disproportionate reactions of intense attraction, but along with it, fear of rejection that you may not have experienced for years. And yet you were convinced those feelings were long gone.

That is why trying to convince yourself to let go of the past on an intellectual level alone may not be a sufficiently effective strategy for healing and moving ahead. The self-sabotaging past may actually be lying dormant in us and in order to combat it we may have to use creative, unique and effective methods to let it go.

Many don't like to admit these things and often spend a lot of energy trying to keep the outside world from seeing their authentic self. They work very hard at creating an image for the world, due to an extreme preoccupation with what others think of them. Sooner or later, however, the facade will likely be revealed for what it is. Those committed to self-development usually accept and understand that as part of personal growth, having the humility and courage to admit that change is essential. Rather than accepting it as a weakness, they view it as a sign of strength to admit it, embrace it and grow from it.

So where does the negativity come from? Well, some of our past negative experiences may have to do with family members or others who played significant roles in our lives such as friends, teachers and/or lovers. The emotions of anger, sadness and fear are the most powerful emotions that we tend to hold onto around these relationships; most often the pain and hurt we feel involves people closest to us.

Many have trouble letting go of the negative past, and may seek help in the form of counseling, and in more extreme cases, psychiatric help. These methods are sometimes helpful and even necessary; however, I would say in most cases the average person can learn to let go of emotional baggage and grow as a person by using simple and highly effective methods on their own. One method that I teach some of my clients for letting go of the past is through what I call **"Power Healing Letters."** There are two types of healing letters. One has to do with forgiving others for some past pain or hurt and the second is about forgiving yourself for being so hard on YOU all these years.

Power Healing Letters

This exercise has proven to be one of the most effective ways for letting go some of the negative effects of our negative past. The purpose of this letter is to help you neutralize the self-limiting feelings you may still harbor toward others. If you have already thoroughly forgiven others from your past, then this exercise may be useful by passing it on to others who may need it. For those of you who continue to harbor resentment toward one or more individuals, I highly recommend that you complete this exercise before moving on. The first step is to identify one person from your past, preferably the person that had the most negative impact on you.

Please note this is not a letter that you would actually physically send to another person, although you may send it if you feel it is the right thing to do. I must emphasize that this exercise of forgiveness is being done not for the other person's sake, but for *your* sake. You don't have to like someone to forgive them, but you have to forgive them in order to like yourself!

In fact, the person you are writing to may even be deceased. The only time you would actually send the letter or communicate your forgiveness verbally would be when you truly felt it would be an empowering, freeing and appropriate thing for you to do, and for the other to receive. Let's begin writing the letter. (Please remember that the following words are only samples. In order to have full impact you need to write the letter in *your* own words).

Paragraph #1

Dear _____ ,

"*I hope all is well. Just letting you know that I am embarking on a self-development journey and one of the things I am learning about is how significant relationships I have had in the past have impacted me both negatively and positively and you are one of those people. I do appreciate the positive impact you had in areas like_____. At the same time, I have also harbored negative thoughts and feelings toward you for a number of* reasons. *The purpose for this letter is for me to finally clear the air and forgive you".*

It is important to remember that this is only a sample idea of how you connect with the person in the first paragraph. You should communicate in a way that is appropriate for you and makes you feel comfortable.

Paragraph #2

This is where you clear the air. It is important to remember that this part of the exercise is about acknowledging, owning and expressing your feelings, and <u>not</u> about criticizing or "dumping" on the other person. It is a time for you to acknowledge how you have felt over the years. For example:

> *I want you to know that I was very angry when you...*
>
> *I was very hurt when you...*
>
> *I was very disappointed when you...*
>
> *I was extremely sad when you...*

You keep writing until you have nothing else to say...

It may include things they did or neglected to do. Once you complete the "clear the air" exercise, you can go on to paragraph *#3.*

Paragraph #3

The following is a sample:

> *I am now giving you back all the feelings of guilt, pain, sadness, etc.*

While you are writing, you imagine sending back all of these unwanted thoughts and feelings to that person, and then you write, *"I now completely forgive you for everything you did or did not do that had a negative impact on me in the past and I wish you well!"*

Please remember that you are forgiving that person for your sake, not theirs. You may never see them again, but you are simply letting go of the inner "infection" that you have allowed to fester within you all these years.

Now that the first letter is complete you can begin thinking about any other person from your past that you also feel the need to write a similar letter to. If you do, then simply follow the exact format as the first one. If not, then you are ready for part 2 of the exercise which is to write a letter to yourself. In many cases, people have forgiven others, but continue to suffer because they have not forgiven themselves for being so overly self-critical. One of the most common issues I have seen over the years is that far too many people are way too hard on themselves. And so, as much as it is important to forgive others, it is equally important to forgive ourselves. So with a pen and paper, begin writing a letter to your little inner boy or girl.

Dear Little John/Jane,

The first paragraph is written in a very similar fashion to the one you did in the first exercise. The second paragraph is a little different as you replace the "clearing the air" paragraph with an apology paragraph. The following are only examples of the way you would apologize for specific issues. Again these are just samples and you are encouraged to do your own that relate specifically to *your* past.

I want you to know little John that I apologize for not pursuing your dream career.

I apologize little Jane for not respecting your body.

I apologize for not attracting more fun filled and nurturing relationships.

I apologize for not building up your self-confidence.

I apologize for neglecting you in so many ways.

I apologize for being overly critical toward you at times.

Continue apologizing until you have nothing left to apologize for.

Once you've completed this section, you go on to write, as you visualize yourself giving that little boy or girl a big hug, for example:

I am now asking you to forgive me for all the things I did or did not do, that negatively impacted your life.

I just want you to know that I accept you, respect you and love you unconditionally like my very own little boy/ girl and I am now committed to giving you the very best in every area of your life!

Completing these power healing letters will likely make you feel lighter, happier and more peaceful. One of my Skype clients from California literally glowed one day after doing this exercise. A weight was lifted and she was able to fast track her growth over the next few months.

Another exercise for letting go of the negative past is done through 'self-talk'. Keep in mind that our words and speech come first and foremost from our thoughts. Often in undisciplined ways, we blurt out words that are at times inappropriate and even harmful, and more often than not, they are a reflection of how we actually feel about ourselves. As we become more aware of these negative patterns, we can be more effective at transforming the negative thoughts into constructive and positive ones. Here's an example:

Let's say that you have a pattern of thinking something like, "I just can't ever see myself speaking in front of a large group of people." Now we know that currently you may find it a challenge to do so, but that statement, "I *can't ever see myself speaking in front of a group,*" is a clear affirmation and belief that you are quite committed to. It is important to be aware of how much energy you are actually giving to that negative belief.

That is just one more example of a negative virus in your inner software. You would never accept viruses to take hold of your computer, so why are you not as horrified when you continue to allow inner viruses to sabotage your inner computer? One little exercise to do is every time you notice you are about to speak out a negative thought, stop yourself and say firmly aloud or silently, as if you were talking to an unwanted guest, "thank you for sharing that, but I'm not really interested," and then get back on track living the moment with complete presence of mind and life purpose.

Another part of letting go of the past is learning to release toxic relationships which may be undermining your growth. As you commit to yourself more and more, you will naturally see the need to let go of those things that undermine your life, and conversely, take on things that empower your life.

Sometimes the process of letting go can be somewhat painful, partly because we might not want to disappoint others or we may simply miss some of the bad habits we cling to because we are so darn accustomed to them. However, if we keep our Vision and Purpose top of mind we will likely develop the courage to let go and cultivate a strong determination to move forward. We then find a whole new world opens up to us, and we are in a much more formidable position to truly manifest what we want out of life.

Connect with your Past - Overview

In this chapter, we addressed the issues from our past which continue to sabotage our growth, development and success. We observed that these issues live inside us like "inner parasites" and that we need to flush them out thoroughly as possible in order to move forward with our lives. A number of exercises were recommended to forgive others, as well as forgiving yourself for being so hard on you all these years. Although this stage of the process is not much fun, it is such a critical foundation to our personal and lifestyle growth. Going to the dentist is not fun, but we often feel good when we leave knowing the problem is behind us. This step should take one to two hours to complete, depending on how many letters you need to write.

The following are common questions we receive about *Connect with your Past.*

Q. ***I just have such a hard time forgiving some of the people from my past. What they did to me bordered on evil. I just cannot think of them in any positive way.***

A. Forgiving others has nothing to do with thinking of them in a positive way. You let go because you recognize that harboring hate and anger toward another person, however despicable they may be, only serves to poison your own mind and heart. The act of forgiveness is done for *your* sake, not for the other person's sake. You may never see them again and you may not like them. It really doesn't matter. The purpose of forgiveness is about releasing your own resentment and anger so that you no longer allow the *memory* of that person or their actions to continue to rob you of your inner peace, happiness and success in life.

Q. ***I find that certain people in my life drag me down. How do I solve this?***

A. Take note that your language, *"they drag me down,"* is an example of victim language, not the language of empowerment. You are actually giving these people way too much power and the way you think and speak about it indicates a lot more about *you* than it does about them. In reality, they don't drag you down. Rather you allow yourself to indulge in negative thoughts and feelings around the negative experience of dealing with these people.

In every one of these experiences you actually have a choice of how you respond or react to them. As you commit to self mastery and self responsibility you may actually welcome these challenges because they provide you opportunities to *respond* rather than *react* to difficult people and circumstances. An empowering way to deal with this is to say, *"When I am around these people, I feel sad or down momentarily; however, I make the commitment to pick myself up by the inner bootstraps and get back into the zone and back on track with me."*

Victor Frankl a psychologist who lived in the Nazi concentrations camps had an attitude that said, *"They can take away my physical freedom but cannot take away my inner freedom."* If Frankl can display such self-mastery within those extreme conditions, surely we can do the same with annoying and difficult people in our lives.

Q. **What happens if the person I need to forgive is not alive?**

A. It doesn't really matter whether the person is alive or not, your negativity about them is alive. Again, this exercise is primarily for *you*, not them. You are simply releasing unwanted thoughts and emotions around your past experiences with that person and you always have a choice to either be a victim of or a master of them. Either we go down the path of self-righteousness and convince ourselves that we are totally justified in resenting this person, or we take responsibility for our own disproportionate reactions and move on. At the end of the day, we either commit to being RIGHT or we commit to being FREE.

Q. **I feel like I have forgiven several times in my life, but the resentment keeps coming back. What can I do?**

A. Again, I remind you that there are 9 steps to this process. Forgiveness by itself will not provide you the freedom you seek. That is why this step is followed by Vision and Purpose in step #3, Inner Fitness in step #4 and Action and Accountability in step #5. However important it is to replace some of the negative and self-destructive thoughts and emotions with positive ones, it is equally important to build a very healthy sense of self-confidence and self-esteem to protect us from ever letting the "parasites" of resentment return.

Feelings of resentment toward another often relates to the anger we have toward ourselves for not living the life we truly aspire to using the other as an excuse or scapegoat. People who feel content, happy and successful in their lives generally have very little reason or room for holding onto resentment toward others.

Q. *It seems unrealistic that all our negative past will go away. I would love you to comment.*

A. The goal is not to eliminate the past completely be it in the form of memories or unwanted feelings. The goal here is to limit the negative impact that we allow these thoughts and feelings to have over us. The goal of the "letting go" process is to *minimize*, not necessarily to completely eliminate them. Most of us can relate to a time in our lives when we have been in an "accident" that made us look physically disfigured. However gross it may look to others in the beginning, after a certain period of healing, the scar may only have a minor impact on how we look. It became an almost invisible wound from the past that does not significantly diminish our appearance in the present. In fact, it might even add to the overall character of how you look.

Q. *I could never forgive my mother for all the despicable things she did to us. How can I even begin to forgive her? It feels impossible.*

A. By your comment it sounds like you believe that if you forgive your mother, somehow you will let her off the hook. That's not what forgiveness is all about. What she did might have been terrible, but forgiving her is about *letting go* of the poison of resentment that lies within you. It has become a totally different issue that is more about your self-mastery and inner peace, and not about the things you despise about her.

Step #3 Connect With Your Vision

"Achievement is largely the product of steadily raising one's levels of aspiration and expectation."

—*Jack Nicklaus, My Story*

Now that you have a better idea of you current life condition and have neutralized some of your negative past, it is a great time to envision the type of life you truly wish to live. You might ask, *"Why is it so important to have vision and purpose?"* Well, "how do you get to a specific destination if you don't know what your plan is?" And how do you get to that destination if you don't muster up the commitment to make it happen.

Vision and purpose means having a vision and a strong commitment to make that vision come to reality. For example, if you decide to take a trip somewhere, don't you need to choose where you would like to go before you decide how you're going to get there. That is why most companies place great importance in having a company "**mission statement**." But they also have a *plan of action*.

Having a clear company vision helps rally the team around having a common goal that everyone can enthusiastically and cooperatively work toward. It gives everyone a sense of purpose, direction and a sense of achievement as they strive toward the bigger goal. In the same way, we too can benefit by having our own personal mission statement for our lives. Having a clear personal vision helps to rally our own troops; our mind, emotions, actions and inner spirit; collectively aligning ourselves toward achieving our lifestyle goals. With the foundation of a clear vision, we can then mobilize ourselves into action and achieve ultimate success. Keep in mind that there is a distinction between what we call vision and small day to day goals to be covered later in step #5, called *Connect to Your Actions.* For now, we will focus primarily on the big vision.

We often hear the expression, *"write down your goals."* This is especially important when we are talking about very short-term daily or weekly goals, but when it comes to the bigger picture; the process generally has a lot more impact if it adds a visual dimension as opposed to merely articulating it in words. What we are finding is that the visual experience actually plays a key role in attracting what we want out of life, even more powerfully than the rational mind does.

As I have already said, way too often in motivational jargon today we hear about how *"knowledge is power"* and how important positive thinking is. That is true to a degree, but I believe we often leave out the important role that the human heart plays in attracting and achieving what we want out of life.

So what can we do to enhance the visioning process so that it will have maximum impact? One powerful exercise is something I call the **"impact visioning process"**. In my years as a coach an trainer it never ceases to amaze me how powerful this very simple and almost childlike exercise can be. So often we think that solutions need to be complex. That may be true in some areas like when you are doing an in-depth scientific study or when pursuing a career as a doctor. However, when it comes to the pursuit of self-development, most often the answers and solutions are simple. It is so liberating to get our busy rational minds out of the way and get back to living with creativity, presence of mind and self mastery.

This impact vision board can be done either alone or within a group of like-minded people who are on the same page and ready to commit to raising the bar in their lives. You can simply purchase a poster board from a local pharmacy and use it as your backdrop for all the pictures and cut outs you will place on it. The first step in the process is to do a brainstorming exercise. You can begin the process now by writing down what you would like to achieve in the following areas over the next few years:

1. Physical Health and Fitness
2. Financial Freedom
3. Career Path
4. Relationships
5. Time Management
6. Education
7. Fun, Leisure and Adventure
8. Spirituality
9. Professional Skills
10. Social Responsibility

Begin by gathering images from magazines, personal photos and any other trinkets that will reflect visually what you would like to attract and create for yourself in every area of your life. You may wish to place a personal photo of yourself in the middle of the vision board to have a constant reminder that *you* alone are responsible for creating the life you wish to live.

If you are a religious or spiritual person you may choose to have an object of your faith in the middle to reflect the precedence of the spiritual dimension; however, you may still choose to place a picture of yourself close by as a reminder that you are co-operating with spirit to attract what you want out of life.

I encourage you to accumulate as many pictures and words that reflect your goals and dreams. You can place them onto the board in a circular fashion like a collage all of which reflects your dream lifestyle including your short-term, medium-term and long-term goals. Allow your mind to freely imagine the big picture of what you would like to attract and create. As you flip through the pages of your favorite magazines, cut out any picture that jumps out at you and is in alignment with your vision. Keep cutting and pasting until you have a pretty complete picture of your desired life. It is important that it have what we call a "WOW factor," and if it does not have that factor, then you didn't do the exercise properly. When you look at your impact vision board, it should invoke the feeling of "WOW - this is an amazingly exciting vision". You should feel very pumped and committed to making it all happen. One of my clients from New York is a graphic artist and she literally created her vision board connecting two walls in her room. I was blown away by the impact it had on me when she texted me the photo. That's how powerful this fun exercise can be. Many of my other clients have gone on to figure out simple ways to do their vision boards online and use it as their desktop display.

Remember many of us get bogged down with day to day details of life and sometimes lose track of our bigger picture vision and passion. Doing the impact vision board exercise not only clarifies your vision, but also serves as a daily visual reminder of the importance of living each day to the fullest with the bigger picture goal in mind. As you clarify the vision and purpose, your motivation and passion for life gets stronger, which in turn helps to enthusiastically commit to doing all the little things you need to do every day to make it all happen.

I recommend you place your board somewhere prominent, either in your home or workplace. It will serve as a constant reminder of what means the most to you. It will also help to remind you of the importance of who you really are and the importance of being proactive in pursuing your vision. Your board should not be something static and do feel free to add or remove images as it is important to keep that "WOW" feeling fresh, current and alive.

There will come a time when you will sense the need to create a brand new "impact vision board". Having a clear and exciting vision is so important to our personal development as it sets a solid foundation for all the steps that follow. Having a clear vision is like laying the cement groundwork for which you are now ready to build the superstructure called living an extraordinary life. Steps #1, 2 and 3 are relatively easy to do and can be done quite quickly. For some people it may take a day and for others a week or so. Now the heavy lifting begins. Now we have to strengthen our inner self-confidence and mental toughness in order to jump start our ability to achieve the exciting vision we just designed for ourselves.

Connect with Your Vision - Overview

In this chapter you learned to exercise your visioning muscles. It began by doing a brainstorming exercise to help unleash your intuition and insights related to your desired lifestyle. As you go through the process you will be able to distinguish and connect the longer term goals with the shorter term goals and also be ready to create your own "impact vision board". You will learn how to create it by using words and pictures, all of which, when meshed together, help create the "WOW" factor and mirror the life you truly wish to live on all levels. I recommend you take a full week to brainstorm and create a truly memorable "impact vision board".

The following are common questions we receive about discovering your vision and purpose:

Q. ***I don't really know what my vision is. How can I gain clarity?***

A. One exercise that might help you is to set simple goals, one at a time. For example, start with physical fitness and write down a goal, perhaps losing or gaining weight. Then do the same with every area of your life. Before you know it your creative juices kick in and you then have a foundation for creating a great impact vision board. You are then ready to get a poster board and begin painting a picture of your desired lifestyle.

Q. ***Is it realistic to focus primarily on my business goal and put my personal life on hold? Or is it more important to go more slowly and schedule time for everything?***

A. It could be either. A balance between personal and business life is always recommended. True success often begins with having a healthy approach to a balanced life. Having said that, there are times when you have to focus on achieving a goal with a specific short term deadline, and may require sacrificing other things. As long as you don't stay imbalanced for too long of a period, this time of sacrifice may be necessary. If you are not careful though, there is always a danger of a buildup of too much stress with potential "burn out" implications. Having said that, when you do focus on a goal for a period of time, it does not necessarily mean abandoning yourself completely. You can still take time for yourself each day, even if only a short period of time. It is so easy to put ourselves on the back burner, so stay vigilant and never forget *you* are number one!

Q. *Can I do my impact vision board on my desktop?*

A.   You can have an impact vision board wherever you like. The purpose is to have access to a constant visual reminder of what you want to attract and achieve in life. The only one guideline for the board is that it must have a **WOW** factor. You should be able look at it and feel genuine excitement. So you can certainly do yours on your desktop. Be creative and when it comes to vision, feel free to let your imagination run wild.

Q. *How often do I do an impact vision board?*

A.   Again that is totally up to you. Creating an impact vision board is not a static exercise. You may add and remove things until you get to the stage when you are ready to create a whole new one. Our lives change, as do our goals so doing a new board may be totally appropriate. My experience is that most people know exactly *when* to do that. Your intuition will guide you.

Q. *Sometimes I am reluctant to do exercises like this because they seem so 'pie in the sky'. They are nice dreams, but don't seem rooted in reality. Why should I see this exercise any differently?*

A. If the program ended here you would be right, as doing an impact vision board would simply be a "pipe dream". That is precisely why this is a 9-step program and not a 3-step program. It can only work effectively if you do the entire program. Having a clear vision is only a foundation of what is to come, and this vision must have a strong emotional commitment and strategic action plan.

Q. *Once I complete my impact vision board, how do I most effectively use it?*

A. I recommend that you put it either in a prominent place in your home or office so that you have a constant reminder of it during the day. Some people put it in their closet and actually hide it in order to avoid ridicule from family members who may not understand or appreciate the significance of the exercise. They then take the vision board out specifically when doing their daily inner fitness exercises. You can do it in whatever way you feel comfortable as the goal is have a constant reminder of what your dream is and to never let go of that dream.

Q. *I am so confused about what I really want to do career-wise, so how do I gain clarity?*

A. Brainstorming often works really well to clarify your career path. Using pen and paper, make a list of about twenty to thirty possible careers, irrespective of whether you are attracted to them or not. Once the list is complete, assess how passionate you are about each one by giving them a score from 1-10, 1 being least passionate, 10 being the most passionate. Then create a shortlist of those careers in your top six. As you observe the choices, some may emerge as a nice fantasy but not really part of reality now or ever. An example of that is if you are forty-five years old and want to be a professional football player. That would not be part of reality, although it may reflect a passion for sports that you could fulfill in another way, like being a sports journalist or an announcer. As you ponder your shortlist, you will likely see two or three categories emerge that trigger your true career passion. Then make a list of all the things you love about that type of work. Once your vision gets clearer, you can decide if this is a career you can begin right away or if it is more long-term, something you need to work toward in the future. Even if it's for two to three years down the road, having done this exercise, will provide you with a clearer vision of what you really want long term and may help you stay motivated in your current job, now that you see the more exciting bigger picture.

Q. *Why is doing an impact vision board so important?*

A. Having a vision is important in order to know where you are going in life both professionally and personally. Vision comes before action. If we lack vision, we might be spinning our wheels for a long time remaining off track from our desired destination. Creating an "impact vision board" not only defines your direction and goals, but also includes the visual dimension which should provide you with that emotional incentive to go out and make it happen. It is our emotions and our passion that really propel us into action. In a nutshell, creating an impact vision board introduces a motivational aid that ignites our determination and emotional commitment toward achieving our goals.

Step #4 Connect With Your Inner Power

"Toughness is in the soul and spirit, not in muscles."

—Alex Karras

In step #2, we learned how to neutralize the negative past. Some people, however, have wrongly assumed that once they have forgiven someone, all will be fine once and for all. Letting go of the negative past is great but unless you replace it with a healthy dose of life-affirming beliefs, attitudes and actions, there is always the danger that the old negative patterns may re-surface to haunt us once more.

Over the years a number of clients have told me that even though they had forgiven someone from their past, the resentment and anger never completely went away and at some point in their lives, it began to reappear quite strongly. That is precisely why step #4 is so vital, as it is all about strengthening our inner core. It is where we replace the negativity from the past, with the positive mindset by strengthening our lives from the inside out. We'll learn to cultivate such things as having a calm and clear mind, being mentally tough, and emotionally strong. Happiness and success in life begins with having a deep sense of true inner fitness and personal power.

There are an abundance of books available today that speak about the power of positive thinking and few would deny the role it plays in our overall mental health. However, in my experience as a coach, I have found that positive thinking by itself has less impact than you might think. Being fit on the inside is about much more than positive thinking because our inner world also includes our emotions, intuition and our heart, our soul or what I call being in the **zen zone**. In fact, when it comes to self-empowerment, more and more experts believe the heart is in fact even more powerful than the rational mind. (www.heartmath.org)

It would be somewhat irresponsible for me as a coach to encourage positive thinking methods to some people, who may not yet be at a stage where these methods alone would even work effectively. If your goal is to hike up Mount Everest, and you are in poor physical condition, would it be responsible to encourage you to climb up the whole mountain right away? Of course not! You would need to spend considerable time getting into the right physical shape in order to accomplish that feat. Attempting to do it prematurely could not only cause injury but also diminish your motivation toward ever attempting it again.

Then why are so many people recommending that you climb the inner Mount Everest through "rah rah" seminars and simplistic affirmations when you may not have the sufficient inner power to accomplish the goal? That is why I insist on a step by step process so each individual progresses one step at a time to ensure a safe journey and long term success.

It is important to understand and achieve all the steps that go into attaining a high level of self-mastery and to go through them in a methodical fashion. When you get to step #7 and learn about "Connecting with Your Magnetism", you will get a better idea of why this more advanced step needs to be founded on the more fundamental and basic inner fitness exercises that we address here in step #4. In this chapter, we will cover the basic exercises you need in order to build up your inner strength as a solid foundation for taking on the more advanced turbo charged inner power training you will experience later on.

We all have a rational mind in order to think, we have human emotions in order to feel, we have intuition to access instinct, wisdom and insights, and we have a heart which allows us to tap into a higher source. Some people might call it spirit or soul but for simplicity sake I will refer to it here as simply the "heart" or the zen zone.

The left brain rational mind refers to the flow of thoughts we have during any given day. These include thoughts like, "I wonder what I'm going to eat this morning?" or "I'm really excited about the trip we're taking this weekend," or "I don't know if I'm up to doing that." Be it simple thoughts like these or more profound ones, we are referring here to the linear analytical mind that plays an important role in our lives. Some people have a more hyperactive mind than others, but all of us without exception experience an abundance of rational thoughts every day.

The emotions simply refer to the full range of feelings we experience such as fear, anger, sadness, frustration, insecurity; as well as passion, excitement and enthusiasm. Our intuition refers to deep insights and instincts which help guide us in our creativity and decision making. Tapping into our intuitive nature is much easier to access when our mind is still, as opposed to being hyperactive and stressed out.

The "heart" refers to that quiet, calm, peaceful, inner joyful and compassionate state that psychologists call the "alpha state". Whether we are conscious of it or not, it dwells deep inside us just like the blue sky always lies beyond the cloud formations that may temporarily block its view. Some people are hardly aware of the power of the heart because they are constantly bombarded by rational thoughts or emotional turbulence.

Others may enjoy glimpses of it and still others are aware of its presence most of the time. In order to achieve a high level of inner fitness, it is important that we have the mind, emotions and intuition and heart all working together, preferably with the heart leading the way. Now that we have identified the different aspects of our inner world, it's time to look at what we can do on a daily basis to increase the fitness level of each area.

THE RATIONAL MIND

We begin with the rational mind by looking at three categories:

- Category #1 refers to positive and life affirming thoughts
- Category #2 refers to a hyperactive stream of random thoughts
- Category #3 refers to negative self-programming thoughts

When I speak of the rational mind I do understand that some people are more visual than verbal, and relate more to the term "imaginations" which are merely the act of picturing our words. For the sake of simplicity I will refer to thoughts and imaginations as the rational mind.

Category #1 is all about the positive use of the rational mind. If you want to set goals or gain more knowledge, then using the rational mind can be extremely valuable and beneficial. If you are in school or simply wanting to learn more about a specific subject, then gathering information on that subject makes you more aware and insightful. Also, if you spend some time on clarifying your vision in life or setting tangible goals, the thinking process involved in that exercise can be extremely beneficial and useful. That's how the rational mind was meant to be used. However, it is important to remember that like anything else, the rational mind can be misused. It can become our master rather than our servant and that is when problems can arise.

Category #2 refers to hyperactive thinking which is when you think or fantasize too much and experience very little calmness, inner peace and overall mental clarity. The constant inner chatter not only limits your experience of inner freedom, but also may create emotional stress, stifle your creative thinking and generally cloud your overall awareness level. So learning to decrease hyperactive thinking becomes an important part of achieving a high level of inner fitness and self mastery. That means having a healthy functioning mind that is not spinning out of control with obsessive thought and images, but rather, one that is free to think clearly, access intuition and respond effectively with others.

Category #3 refers to negative programming, that may have rooted in early childhood. This is when we have specific thought patterns that are self-defeating and influence how we feel, act and communicate with others. These negative patterns are like having infections in the mind, likened to a computer that may have viruses that must be eliminated from the program. An inner de-frag is in order!

So we begin our journey inward starting with the rational mind. For the purpose of this exercise I would like you to think of the thing you most dislike about yourself. Think about what your biggest weakness might be and I am not talking here about something you cannot change like for example your height. Think of that one thing about yourself that if you could only change, would have a major impact in your life. It could be for example procrastination, impatience or lack of confidence. It can be anything at all, so as we go through this exercise, choose whatever issue is most appropriate for you at this time.

Using pen and paper, draw a line right down the middle of a blank page. On the top of the left column, write the word "AFFIRMATION" and on the top of the right side, write the word "REACTION." Most of you should be familiar with the term "affirmation" as it usually refers to a positive statement or confirmation about something you wish to have, experience or feel. Affirmations are generally repeated over and over silently.

However helpful this approach may be, I recommend the following 3 part approach to affirmations which also includes verbal expression and physical action. The chances of a successful outcome are much greater if you have all 3 parts working together as it becomes a more complete and practical approach to an affirmational exercise. If you are a more visual person, as you write down your affirmations on paper, take a second or two imagining yourself visually experiencing what you are writing. The funny thing is in reality we are doing affirmations all the time. Unfortunately many of them are negative, useless thoughts and even self-destructive.

Some examples might be:
∷ *Oh, I'll do that tomorrow.*
∷ *Oh, I'll do that tomorrow.*
∷ *I'm not good enough.*
∷ *If only someone loved me.*
∷ *I can't afford that.*
∷ *I will never have that.*
∷ *I am a loser.*

These are only a few of many other similar thoughts that we may experience repeatedly every day. Transforming negative thinking into positive requires some discipline and commitment, and that is why doing some formal exercise like the following one can be very valuable.

In the left column I suggest you write out a positive affirmation connected to your issue: in this case, procrastination. So the affirmation can be, *"I take action right away."* Yes I know, you are saying something you don't really believe, but that is exactly how we will transform the negative into a positive. Begin by writing that same statement over and over down the left hand column of the page. Every time you complete the affirmation on the left side, if you observe any positive or negative thoughts, write them down on the right hand column. Immediately return to writing out the positive affirmation on the left side, and if there are any positive or negative thoughts, write them down on the right side. If there are no thoughts then simply continue writing the positive affirmation down the left side.

There are three stages to this exercise. The first we call the *resistance* stage where you will likely notice a lot of negative thoughts showing up on the right hand side. Your comfort zone is being threatened and the negative army of thoughts or images you're used to giving attention to, won't really like the new found positive thoughts you are now affirming on the left side. Expect some pretty strong resistance during this stage. It might look like this:

I take action right away....Ridiculous

I take action right away....No way

I take action right away....B.S.

I take action right away....What a stupid exercise

As you continue the exercise, you will notice a shift in the quality of thoughts down the right side. The negative thoughts begin to weaken in intensity because you are now giving equal attention to the positive re-enforcement. Instead of reactions like "no way" or "ridiculous" or "not true" you will begin to experience reactions more like, "we'll see" or "maybe." In stages, the negative reactions begin to weaken in their power which is why we call it the **weakening** stage.

The final stage is called the **power** stage, now as you write out the affirmation, you begin to feel the impact of the affirmation with a very powerful conviction in your heart. At that point you no longer write anything down the right side, as you focus all of your attention on writing the affirmation in the left column six times. Remember to press your pen hard down on the paper with strong conviction and emotion, thus imprinting the new affirmation deeper into your conscious and subconscious mind. At that point you have completed the writing part of the exercise. Now you are ready to channel the words into a strong emotional commitment. I recommend you do this part of the exercise standing up, as it often adds to your conviction level.

Begin to verbalize your affirmation with passion from your gut for about two to three minutes. "I TAKE ACTION RIGHT AWAY... I TAKE ACTION RIGHT AWAY, I TAKE ACTION RIGHT AWAY"... making sure that you verbalize it from your gut and not your throat. Many professional tennis players today will grunt as they are about to hit the ball because it results in a more intense impact in their swing. The grunt sound comes from an area slightly below your navel. By placing your attention there, you are able to channel your emotions much more powerfully than if it came from your throat.

What you are doing is taking the affirmation out of the mind and igniting the much needed emotional element, preparing yourself for the third part of the exercise which is to translate all of this into action. Once you complete the verbal part, I recommend taking action right away, for at least twenty minutes or longer. It is important to plan out what specific action you'll take before beginning the entire exercise that day, as it is preferable that there be no delay going from one part of the exercise to another. For example, in this case related to procrastination, the action could be that you go directly to the kitchen and clean up all the dishes that have piled up over the last few days. The action part of the exercise should be at least twenty minutes long but if you choose to go longer that is just fine. Once you have completed all three stages of the exercise you will likely feel more clear minded, focused and motivated.

Please remember that procrastination is only one example of an issue you can choose to address. Others may include such things as patience, fear of rejection, laziness, diet, money, relationships; anything that resonates with *you*. Once you have successfully done this exercise with one of your self- limiting patterns, you can then use the same exercise with any other issue you wish to address. This will help you to transform your negative thinking into positive thinking.

The key is do these exercises regularly, sometimes for days, weeks or even months until the results become fully entrenched as part of you. For best results, I recommend you the writing, verbal and action parts for two days, and then day 3-7 you can eliminate the writing part by only doing the verbal and action part. After one solid week of doing this exercise you can then plan the following week to redo the same affirmation or choose another one that you would like to master at this time.

THE EMOTIONS

Like the rational mind, our human emotions can be used to enhance our lives or sabotage it. The emotions are connected to the mind in a mutually reciprocal way. For example, if you just graduated from university you would more than likely feel emotions of joy and excitement along with positive thoughts about yourself. Both your mind and emotions would be working in harmony, the way they should. On the other hand if you were just rejected by a person you are in love with, your emotions of hurt and sadness would likely influence your thoughts in a negative way. Our rational thoughts are like our own computer programming while our emotions are more like the combustion and generator that propel us into action and communication with others. They can also serve as warning signals to protect us from danger, or enhance our communications through passion, enthusiasm and affection.

That is why in the previous 3 part affirmation exercise, it is recommended to include the second part of verbalizing your affirmation. You will also see in the following "heart power" exercise why I recommend including verbal expression, as it often helps to channel and strengthen your positive emotional muscles.

Some people live primarily in their head guarding their emotions, while others may wear their emotions on their sleeve, ignoring the rational parts. Either one of these extremes can cause inner turbulence within us and negatively influence our actions and relationships with others. The point of this chapter is to understand that by calming and centering your mind, by re-programming negative beliefs, by learning to channel your emotions and by connecting with your heart, you can begin to live with a much greater level of *inner freedom*. As a result, your life becomes a lot simpler, happier and much more productive.

THE ZEN ZONE

Now we are ready to look at a part of our inner world that goes beyond thought, emotion and intuition. There are many words used to describe it; ranging from clear mind, big mind, peace of mind, or the source. It is probably more important to focus on the benefits of accessing this state than it is to name it, but I will refer it as getting into our "heart or zen zone". With all the changes going on in the world, our fast paced lives, and with the emergence of social media, never has it been more important to balance our lives and ground ourselves.

Being in the "zen zone" is like being *home*. It's where we feel calm, clear and centered as well as content, happy and compassionate. Isn't it amazing how many people experience so little of these inner qualities? Living as a monk for over nine years provided me the opportunity to learn a number of techniques to help me access this part of my inner world.

There are many types of inner fitness exercises. Some are silent in nature while others include sound, and still others focus on physical movement or a combination of all of them. It is important that each person find the appropriate method that works best for them. Once you discover which ones works best for you, try to avoid projecting and preaching to others about it. It's quite astonishing how often people can become attached to their own methods and try to impose or manipulate others into believing that there is no other way.

It is interesting to note that some of my female students have reported benefiting more from dancing ten minutes to their favorite music than in doing some form of silent meditation exercise. Whatever the method is, the goal is simply to tap into your "zen zone" and sustain the benefits for as long as possible. So be careful not to get overly attached to the specific methods as they will vary from person to person.

Most of us associate the term "meditation" with an exercise you do in silence, cross legged and in some form of yoga position. However effective these methods may be for some, they can be quite challenging to others, at least initially. Because of our fast-paced lifestyles we are bombarded with an inordinate amount of external stimulation, and it takes a lot of discipline and self-mastery to still the mind simply by doing a silent form of practice. That is why I recommend to most of my clients a simpler inner fitness exercise that connects to our voice and sound. It not only gets the emotions involved but also does not require any specific physical posture in order to experience results.

The verbal fitness exercises, if done effectively, will help cut through the barrage of rational thought and help you tap into your "zen zone". If you have a specific religious or spiritual inclination, you can certainly replace the words of the verbal exercise to coincide with your beliefs. So in the following exercise, I will give you some suggestions, but feel free to change the words to any combination of words and phrases that make you feel most comfortable, and project for you the most meaning and power. For our purpose here, I will use the following two:

1. **I'm in the ZONE!**
2. **I'm in the FLOW!**

Just repeat these words over and over rhythmically for at least three to five minutes twice a day. In time, as you master it you can increase that to five or ten minutes or longer. Choose an environment that is conducive to doing the exercise, as you will be vocalizing aloud, so it might be wise to have plenty of privacy. Begin by repeating the phrase over and over, not too quickly but not too slowly either.

If done too slowly it allows too much time for thoughts or images to invade your awareness. If done too quickly, it may cause you to fall over your words and stress you out. The best and most effective way is to find a melodic rhythm that has a momentum and makes you feel like you are one with the words. You can also modulate your voice by toning up and down, just like when singing a song. When you run out of breath, simply take a deep inhalation and begin again. I recommend doing it for 2- 3minutes and when you feel more comfortable and skilled at it, you can increase to 10, 15 minutes or longer.

When practiced correctly, it will be like you are experiencing a verbal laser beam of light, so to speak. It will help cut though all the emotional and psychological turbulence, and enable you to tap into that "zen zone" or alpha state where you experience clarity of thought, inner peace and presence of mind. It may take you awhile to get used to doing the exercise properly but once you do, the benefits will be enormous. By practicing it along with the previous affirmational exercises, you will be well on your way to building a solid inner core of inner freedom, mental concentration and self mastery.

If you find that doing the verbal exercise is too challenging, consider alternative methods like taking 3 to 5 minutes to stare at a candle, take up hot yoga or like some of my female clients do, sing and dance to their favorite music for 10 minutes. Remember, the goal is to achieve inner calm and mental clarity, and there are many ways to get there. You simply have to find ways that work for *you*.

Some people prefer a more silent method of calming and centering the mind. If you are one of these, a more simple Zen like practice may be most effective. You can simply sit on the floor propped up on cushions or on a chair, then relax all your muscles, preferably sitting in front of a blank wall about two feet away from you. Looking at the wall with head tilted slightly forward, chin tucked in, begin to count your exhalations silently from one to ten and then repeating that over again for the entire duration of the meditation.

Many of my clients prefer to keep their eyes open and visualize the number on the wall as a visual anchor. You can have a timer next to you so you don't have to keep looking at your watch. You may notice after a short period of time your thoughts begin to increase. It will go something like this: *1-2-3-4-my knee hurts-5-6-7 I'm tired-8-9-10 then back to 1-2-what a stupid exercise-3-4-what will I eat for lunch?* I think you get the picture.

The key to this exercise is to keep coming back to the counting of the breath. As far as your thoughts are concerned, neither try to push them away nor attach yourself to them. Your job is to simply observe the thoughts, coming and going like passing clouds in the sky. Yes it might seem tedious and monotonous at the beginning, however if you consistently do this exercise day after day, week after week sooner or later you will experience a breakthrough into a whole new level of awareness. Your hyperactive thinking will decrease and it will be like finally viewing the big blue sky above the clouds after days of rain, knowing that the blue sky is and was always there. Once you tap into that level of awareness you will likely want to expand the experience more and more into your daily life. Just to clarify, these exercises do not necessarily replace your spiritual exercises. Some people are more religious or spiritual than others. If you are already doing various prayers or meditations that are extremely meaningful and important to you, then the exercises just described in this section can be considered more of a mental and emotional workout, not in any way conflicting with your spiritual beliefs, just as doing physical fitness exercises would not be contradictory to those beliefs.

There are so many benefits to accessing your "zen zone". One is that you will experience much greater levels of mental clarity and concentration. Another is how much more focused you will be during the day. You will begin to access creative thought and intuition, which are such powerful tools to guide you in your life. You will generally feel more grounded and much more in control of your life. One of my clients from Toronto is an executive at large company where the stress levels are off the roof. By doing his inner fitness exercises every day within 30 days not only did he experience less stress at work, but was also much more productive and was able to cultivate better relationships with his staff.

The goal of step #4 is about strengthening your inner core and building up your level of inner fitness. True self-confidence comes first from the inside as we have focused on here in step #4 *and* from your actions and achievements you will experience in step #5. By working on steps #4 and #5 consistently, you will go a long way toward achieving a high level of self-confidence and personal power.

Connect with Your Inner Power - Overview

In this chapter you learned about the important role your inner world plays in achieving what you want out of life. You learned about the difference between the quantity and quality of thoughts, emotions and intuition. You also learned about the "zen zone" and the important role it plays in building up your inner muscles. You learned some basic techniques and exercises which will help you to clear your mind and re-program negative beliefs you might still be holding onto. You were also introduced to some basic inner fitness exercises that will help to prepare you for the next important step which has to do with taking charge of your life.

The following are common questions we receive about Activating your Inner Power:

Q. *How often should I do the "I'm in the Zone" exercise?*

A. I recommend that beginners practice the exercise at least once or twice per day to start, and for at least 3 to 5 minutes each time. It takes a little practice to feel comfortable doing the exercise, as getting into the proper flow is essential in order to experience all of the benefits. Over time you may find that you might wish to extend each session to 10 or even 15 minutes. You may also find great benefits repeating it silently during the day, when there are idle moments like when taking a bus or walking to a specific destination.

Q. *When I try any form of mental concentration exercise, I usually find it very boring. How can I change that?*

A. If you do the exercises properly you will experience a wide range of thoughts, imaginations and feelings; and experiencing feelings of boredom is common. That is natural, however if you persist with the exercise day after day you will ultimately experience more and more moments of peace, mental clarity and joy. In time you will find yourself less attached to passing thoughts and feelings and you will enjoy the benefits of tapping more consistently into the "zen zone".

If after all that, you still don't experience results you may wish to look at your emotions as being the cause as healing emotions are an important foundation for your ability to meditate effectively. All I can say is, keep practicing until you do it effectively. Trust me, as you persist you will go far beyond boredom, and in many cases will want to continue for an hour or more.

Q. *People keep telling me that I need to like myself, but I keep thinking that it is selfish to do so. Am I on the wrong track?*

A. There is a big difference between self-respect and selfishness. Someone who is selfish is a person who is overly self-centered and only thinking primarily about their own needs. These people are usually overly self-serving and generally do not have much concern, respect or compassion for others. Someone who truly respects themselves realizes that having fulfilling relationships with others begins with the one they have with themselves.

With the joy and contentment they begin to feel, they are more able to give their very best to others. Your kitchen cabinet needs to be filled in order to feed your guests. It's all about perspective! Sometimes we confuse giving to others with being a martyr. Having appropriate personal boundaries is certainly a pre-requisite for being a truly loving and giving human being.

Q. *I am thinking of taking a personal coaching program. They all say they can help me, but at the end of the day, how do I really know if it's going to help? I am never 100% convinced. How do I ever really believe it?*

A. If you are waiting for some magical divine-like intervention to come to you to confirm that a specific program is for you, you will be waiting a long time. Ever hear of analysis paralysis? Here's the thing. When you are doing your due diligence in choosing an appropriate person or program, all you can do is get a feel for what type of program they do and get clear on whether their personality and approach resonates with you. Assess whether they are what you are looking for at this time in your life. You can check out testimonials and even contact some of them yourself. After all that you have to let your intuition guide you and just jump in!

Q. *Why is it that every time I try to be positive or take charge of my life, something inevitably happens that ruins my attitude and negatively affects my success?*

A. Your language speaks volumes. Words like "try" and phrases like "it ruins my attitude" all reflect a victim mentality, as if the outside world around you is doing you in. Part of personal growth is becoming aware of the language you use because what you think is what you will likely speak and likely how you will act and communicate. It all begins in the mind. Instead of the word "try," perhaps use a word like "commit," and instead of implying that the external circumstances are "doing you in", instead say, "I experience fear when faced with *such and such* a challenge". And "I am committed to meet the challenge head on anyway". Take complete responsibility for what you think, say, act and ultimately communicate.

Q. *I have tried so hard to think positively but it's so difficult and I don't feel as if it has made that much of a difference in my life. Any advice?*

A. As I say quite often, positive thinking is only one piece of the puzzle. True self-mastery and personal power requires a much broader approach. If somebody says, "I do weightlifting, but it's not helping me to achieve my life goals," it's because weightlifting is only one facet of health in your overall lifestyle. You may consider having a more holistic approach to your journey of self-development.

Step #5 Connect With Your Actions

"If you don't go after what you want, you'll never have it. If you don't ask, the answer is always no. If you don't step forward, you're always in the same place."

—*Nora Roberts*

Ready for step #5? However important having the right mindset is, it is equally important to take action in order to actually create the results we desire. As I said previously, the happiness and success we aspire to comes from both our inner growth and our outer achievements through action. The exercises that you just learned in the previous chapter help you to build a very strong sense of inner freedom and confidence, and now it's time to focus on building the confidence that can only be experienced through ACTION.

I can tell you that the areas of action and time management are the least emotionally appealing areas of personal development. Generally, it is human nature to get excited about doing a vision board, but a pain in the butt to address goals and accountability. We tend to enjoy the fun stuff such as fantasizing our bucket list of dreams, and why not? But truly successful people also understand that dreams without action will simply not work. This is quite evident in today's business world where so many people are now working in some type of home based business; and a common challenge is "discipline". Most entrepreneurs are free spirits by nature, who love to live to the beat of their own drum. They relish their freedom to create their own reality, which often includes visionary qualities of thinking big. At times these same people have the tendency to overlook the annoying smaller details. Being a big thinker myself I have had first hand experience facing this challenge. No matter how exciting and large a persons vision may be, the actual implementation and achievement of that dream usually requires a terrific amount of attention to detail. So if you are an aspiring entrepreneur, beware, because your strength could become your weakness. The excitement of the big picture and attention to detail must go hand in hand in order to ensure long-term success of any project or venture.

Taking consistent action is critical to all of us, both in our business and personal lives. If we are to truly committed to success in all aspects of life, one important factor will always be the importance of taking consistent and prioritized action. Having a clear vision is critical to success. It is the foundation from which all else grows, but unless it is followed by consistent action along with discipline and organization, the vision becomes no more than a flaky dream. I think back to two amazing mentors I have been blessed with in my life, Henry and Stephen.

Henry was the founder of one of the most successful fitness clubs in the country, and I would often pick his brain to learn some of his success secrets. The one most meaningful statement that stands out to me went something like this: "Allan," he would say, "I'm not the fastest or the *quickest man in the world, but I am one of the most determined and focused.*" Henry was on the phone at least four times a day with each and every one of his sales staff, checking in to see if they were on track with their projected sales. He was a kind and fair man, but he understood that the life blood of a successful business came down to results, and that is why focusing on the numbers were critical to his success. Sure, he'd like to motivate and inspire his staff and he often invested in special events to show his appreciation to them, but he also understood that none of this would be possible unless the productivity was achieved.

My other mentor Stephen passed away a number of years ago. I was very fortunate to be his business partner for over ten years. We often joked about him not being my mentor, but rather my '**tor-mentor**'. Stephen was wise and compassionate but, like Henry he understood the bottom line. Yes, if you're a creative and visionary type like I am, better make sure you surround yourself with practical, grounded and successful people. It goes an awful long way toward ensuring that your vision actually becomes a reality.

For example, whenever I allowed myself to get distracted in non-productive activity there was Stephen telling me, *"ALLLLAN, get back to the basics,"* and at that time it meant getting back on the phone to make those boring phone calls. Every time he said that to me, I had such a negative reaction in the pit of my stomach, thinking that I should be beyond having to make those dreaded phone calls. But he was always right. I wanted things to be so much easier and Stephen had a way of bringing me back to reality. At times I wasn't always willing to do the little tasks I needed to do every day to make things happen.

In his book *The E-MYTH*, Michael Gerber talks about how most entrepreneurs actually fail or have mediocre success. There are many reasons for that, but I can tell you first hand that some of the reasons include having a lack of focus, accountability and organization. I often hear successful coaches in the sports world speak about the secrets to winning, and one recurring theme relates to the importance of being attentive to details. The moral of the story is either to develop these organizational skills yourself or if you can afford it, hire people who do have those skills.

So what can we do on a daily basis to become more focused and accountable? One has to do with accountability and the other with prioritization. For accountability, I recommend that my clients use what I call a "Personal Accountability System". It serves as a daily tracking sheet, not to be confused with a daily to-do list, which would include such things as getting a haircut or mailing letters that is, isolated and miscellaneous things that you do one time. The tracking sheet has more to do with ongoing activities in your life that you need to track on a daily or weekly basis in order to achieve your big picture goals. In other words, they refer to activities that you do on a consistent basis either every day or three to four times per week.

If you're in sales, for example, one of your regular activities may be phoning prospective clients. Based on your big picture goal, you then calculate how many contacts on average you need to make every day in order to achieve your goal. Let's say that the number is ten per day. Well, under the category "phone contacts" place the number 10 right across for the next five to seven days. That's your quota.

Every night before you go to bed, fill in the actual number for that day. Then underneath that put the plus or minus of that day. As the week goes by you will have an on-going up to date accumulative plus or minus ratio for the week This not only keeps you accountable to your goals but also gives you a precise up to date reality check, which will help you plan out your next day and your next week. You can do that for every activity you need to focus on at this time either professionally or personally.

To use this system effectively, I recommend focusing on the areas that are most challenging at this time, not ones you have already mastered. During the first week, your main goal may simply be to fill in the tracking sheet, irrespective of the actual results. The initial objective is to get used to filling out the numbers on a daily basis. If you accomplish each goal during your first week, that's a bonus. Most of my clients who do this consistently for 30 days, become increasingly fed up with not staying on track and become ever more determined to take consistent action. It's a simple, yet highly effective tool to help you look in the mirror every day and evaluate your actual accomplishments or lack thereof. It may not be fun, but it works and is highly effective for producing results.

For those of you that still have trouble staying on track after the first week, can institute what I call the **consequence system**. That means that you have an agreement with your success partner who is someone who is willing to support you in achieving your goals. They may or may not be someone who is doing the program. If you don't achieve a specific goal that week, then you will have to do something that will not be very pleasant, such as paying your partner money, in an amount painful enough to dissuade you from a repeat performance. Or it can be something like spending one hour at your friend's house cleaning their home or car. This consequence exercise is only done if you are having trouble disciplining yourself and keeping your word about the goals you set for yourself week to week. Sometimes we need the support of another person in order to kick-start our actions until our discipline comes more naturally from within.

One of my clients from Vancouver is a sales manager and was having trouble keeping his word so we agreed that he would send me a copy of his tracking sheet every day for 30 days. He chose a consequence of paying his son $100 for every day he did not do it. By the second day his son earned $200 because my client didn't send me the sheet, and then for 28 days in a row I received it as I knew I would. He is now a highly focused person.

Another time management tool is the **prioritization** *exercise* which helps you to focus on activities that are most important and conducive to productivity at this time. Nobody wants to spin their wheels getting bogged down in "working harder" instead of "smarter". Most often, entrepreneurs choose to engage in activities that make them feel good, but at times can fool themselves into believing that they are actually being productive. It's a common pattern for people who are more visionary than they are practical. That is why it is so important to ensure that *your* vision is grounded in having a practical step by step plan of action.

Here is a simple way to prioritize. Write down a list of things you need to act on in the short term and long term, leaving nothing out. Brainstorm the list until you run out of things to write down. Then place an A, B, or C next to each one. "A" would represent an activity that is a high priority and needs to be done right away. "B" would represent something you can put off for a few days or a week. "C" would represent things you would like or need to do down the road. Then take all the A's, and list them in order of importance. Begin acting on them the next morning, one by one. Tick off each task as you complete it, so at the end of the day you experience a real sense of achievement. As you proceed, the B's will work up to be A's, and C's will work up to be B's and you can begin to add to a new C list.

By doing both the accountability and prioritization exercises on a consistent basis, day by day you will begin to feel a real sense of streamlining your business and personal life. You'll feel a sense of accomplishment and more than anything, you will begin to achieve the goals you set out to accomplish.

Connect with Your Actions - Overview

In this chapter you learned to distinguish between a daily to-do list and a daily Personal Accountability System, which helps you identify specific categories both personally and professionally that you need to act on every day. You can use quotas and track your actual results by observing the accumulated plus/minus ratios. Each week you and your success partner can help each other be accountable to each other. For those of you who have trouble staying on track, the "consequence system" can be used as a highly effective tool for self generating discipline. The following are common questions we receive about *Connect with Your Actions:*

Q. *As a single working mother of three children, I simply have no time for myself. What do you suggest?*

A. The first thing that I would look at is the use of the term "I have no time." I recommend you change that to "I choose not to take time." Saying you have no time implies you have no choice. I do appreciate that you must be very busy and may not have the leisure or freedom to take much time for yourself. The reality is that millions of people who don't even have children also complain about not having enough time for themselves either. We can always make excuses for why we put ourselves on the back burner. There are always solutions! If you had a crystal ball and saw that in a few years you would burn out or get very sick and be unable to do anything for anyone, you might be more motivated right now to do whatever it takes to seize time for YOU.

Q. *How does a person live life with their focus on their overall goal with balancing the ability to live fully in the present?*

A. It's all about integrating both. You have a goal. You commit to do your daily actions toward achieving that bigger vision goal while being grounded in the present. The most important thing is to remain in the *now* while you're working toward the goal. Then you have the best of both worlds.

Q. *I have tried setting goals so often and although it starts off well, I usually get off track and then give up tracking myself. How do I overcome that?*

A. I recommend having a success partner to keep you accountable. In reality, very few of us are self-directed and disciplined enough to stay on track consistently. That is why it can be quite helpful to access some external support. Find someone who is equally excited about getting to the next level and who is open to the same type of support that you are. Make an agreement with them to chat at least once a week in order to review and set goals and keep each other accountable. You will be amazed at how effective having a success partner can be in helping you stay on track. Think about why most people go to the fitness club to workout rather than doing it at home. One reason may be that it is easier to get motivated when you see so many others doing the same.

Q. *How do I know what goals to put on my tracking sheet?*

A. The tracking sheet is separate from what we would call a daily to-do list. A to-do list for example, might include such tasks as getting a haircut, doing laundry, filling out forms, etc. The tracking sheet on the other hand, is for the sole purpose of tracking key categories of *actions* you need to take, both professionally and personally on a weekly basis. Some of these activities like making phone calls for business may be daily activities while others, such as exercising at the gym, might be done two or three times a week. It's best to select categories that are the most vital for achieving your goals and that you need to be most accountable for.

Q. *What do I do if I fill out the tracking sheet, but week after week I do not really achieve what I set out to do?*

A. The tracking sheet is not just about filling in your goals and quotas. Its main purpose is to help you achieve them. During the first couple of weeks the idea is to simply fill out the sheet irrespective of whether you achieve the goals or not. However, if you find that you are not actually accomplishing your goals, you may have to take more extreme measures like using the *consequence system* with the support of your success partner.

Step #6 Connect With Your Challenges

"Every adversity, every failure, every heartache carries with it the seed of an equal or greater benefit."

—*Napoleon Hill*

Most people who embark on the path of self-development and personal empowerment understand that it won't all be a "bed of roses". We all know there will be obstacles and challenges along the way. One of the more subtle mental traps we can get into, is to have the belief that at a certain point in our inner journey, we reach enlightenment and live in a problem free state of bliss. Of course, most of us veterans know better. As you begin to take consistent action in accordance with your true purpose in life, there is the tendency to imagine that you have *arrived*, have found *the* answer, and that life will magically flow forever. Yeah right! The reality is that life has a funny way of throwing us a series of challenges and obstacles.

Facing these obstacles and challenges will test our progress in so many ways, and quite often we allow ourselves to get off track. The world around us has a funny way of testing us by challenging our true commitment to happiness and success. Did you really expect that by transforming attitudes and beliefs in steps #1 through #5, that your problems would cease to exist? On the contrary, and for this reason I consider this to be one of the most difficult and important stages of the journey toward true self-mastery.

I feel that some of our greatest personal growth and character-building are achieved through the trials and tribulations that we experience in life, most especially by how effectively and masterfully we handle these challenges. Many people succumb to and choose to be victims of the obstacles, while others learn over time to overcome the obstacles by turning them into opportunities for growth. It's amazing how often we allow ourselves to become the victims. Here are some examples you may relate to: *"She broke my heart ..." "His/her attitude brought me down ..."* "The *economy sucks....*" and the list goes on.

These are just a few examples of what we can call victim language. We use language that implies that our suffering is directly caused by something or someone outside of ourselves. In reality, she didn't break my heart. Oh yes, she rejected me and my heart feels pain right now, and of course it is quite natural to feel hurt and sad. However, the key to self-mastery is what we do with that feeling of sadness.

Are we going to blame the other person, beat ourselves up for perceived failure or will take responsibility by lifting ourselves up and get back on track with a positive mindset and joyful spirit? Being rejected by someone however hurtful it may be, actually gives us the opportunity to grow as a person, and move on toward finding a truly fulfilling relationship with someone who actually loves us for the way we are?

Saying words like *"their attitude brings me down"* gives the other person the power: a more constructive thing to say would be, *"I feel upset and angry over having been rejected by that person. However, I choose not to reject myself, I believe in me too much, and I now pick myself up with strong inner resolve to get my life back on track. Now I am ready to attract someone who really likes me for me!"*

People reveal a lot about themselves through the language they use. It is so easy to blame others, however, it takes honesty and courage to take responsibility for our own reactions and commit to mastering the situation, rather than being a victim of it.

Society has evolved to having great mastery over the environment, technology and science, but very little when it comes to conquering the inner workings of our own minds and emotions and in extension our day to day human relationships. It takes great courage to overcome our obsession with the outside world by finally have a heart to heart with the person we see every morning in the mirror. Our obstacles may come from anywhere. They can come through people around us, environmental conditions or through the wily inner workings of our own minds and emotions. How does it feel to be rejected in a relationship? How does it feel to have a flat tire, or be caught in the rain? How does it feel to find out someone we love has cancer or has passed away?

Disappointment, sadness, anger, frustration, and self-doubt are only some of the emotions we can feel when unforeseen events come our way. Many of us allow these emotions to eat away at our inner peace, contentment and joy. We spend more time feeling bad about ourselves than remembering how grateful we should be to be alive, and for all the opportunities that lie just ahead in each and every challenge we face.

The sad part is that many of us live out our whole lives without ever learning to master our thoughts and emotions. Some choose the way of denial by suppressing them, while others go to the opposite extreme by indulging in negativity in an overly overt and disproportionate way. Neither extreme is the real solution to inner self-mastery.

We know for certain that the obstacles and challenges are coming our way whether we like it or not. Sooner or later, "stuff happens", and this is just a fact of life. Some of the challenges will be minor in nature, like the weather changing quickly as we walk outside into unexpected rain. Others will be of medium intensity, like failing an exam, or a major one like being diagnosed with a serious illness.

I have endured many challenges and obstacles along the way just like you have, but the biggest one without exception had to do with my soul mate Suzie, who passed away a few years ago from cancer at the young age of forty-four. I loved her unconditionally for over twenty years, and of course still do. Seeing her suffer over a period of several years was the greatest pain I have endured thus far in my life. My love for her was so deep, and to see her suffer so much, tested every morsel of my self-mastery. And yet I knew I had to practice what I preached. On a daily basis I diligently did my inner fitness exercises that helped me to transform fear into love, and allowed me to stay in a great frame of mind, to be supportive of her as possible.

By staying in this state I not only became free from my own suffering, but was able to maximize the love and support I gave to Suzie during three very challenging years. Through that experience I learned beyond a shadow of a doubt that no matter how difficult our experiences may be, we always have the option of turning the obstacles into opportunities.

Another example of dealing with adversity has to do with the emotions of insecurity and jealousy. Unfortunately, many who experience rejection in a relationship choose the self sabotage path of impulsive reaction. We either lash out at the object of our love and/or turn inward to indulge in our pain with ever mounting self-critical and destructive attitudes. A much more empowering way to deal with this type of pain is to accept that holding on to resentment and anger never ends well. The question is will we indulge in pain or turn it into a timely opportunity for growth? That is always the litmus test. Oh yes, it always hurts to get rejected, but our response to that rejection will either sabotage our life or help us to evolve.

I lived through many rejections myself so I know first hand how self destructive anger turned inward can be. I lived for over 20 years in insecurity about how I looked, how unsuccessful I was and how little confidence I had in relationships. Fortunately for me I had the wisdom to get 'fed up'. I literally got tired of feeling sorry for myself, blaming others and generally in feeling that I was letting my life slip away.

There is another form of obstacle that is much more insidious and powerful than relatively smaller ones, that attack us on a daily basis. Those are fairly easy to recognize and to respond to. This other form is more like a slow-growing inner "cancer" that takes the form of depression, an overall feeling of malaise some might call a darkening of the soul. This type of obstacle envelops our whole being and at times remains with us for long periods of time. Over time we may become aware that something is just not right and cannot always pinpoint the cause.

This is a very normal life experience that may come at different points in our lives. The most effective way to deal with it, is by first and foremost acknowledging that you have a problem. The second is to stop condemning yourself and see that you are being pushed to look deeper inside in order to change something in your life. It might be that you need to shake things up a little, whether it's a change of career, attracting new friends or maybe something more philosophical or spiritual.

Again it all has to do with how we respond to the painful experiences. We can certainly suppress it, try to deny it or to numb it with medication, drugs or alcohol. Some begin obsessing on their work or a specific relationship. Unfortunately, many people see the pain as a sign of weakness or failure and often feel that something is seriously wrong with them. As a result, they are often far too quick in running from themselves, rather than having the courage to face things head on in order to learn the true lessons they are meant to learn.

Some wise teachers from the Eastern traditions, when using the term "enlightenment", are really referring to achieving inner self mastery. It is about experiencing the freedom that comes from dropping our psychological and emotional armor, and by letting go of being overly attached to any people and circumstances around us. The great psychologist Victor Frankl wrote a book about his experiences in the Nazi concentration camps. His attitude was that they could take his physical freedom away, but could not take away his inner freedom. Isn't it interesting that with that attitude and presence of mind, Frankl was one of the few people who actually escaped the concentration camp? Maybe in some way because of his own self-mastery, he was able to focus less on his emotional and psychological anxieties, but more on creative solutions that may have been the key to his escape. If he could accomplish that under such extreme challenges, surely we can all respond similarly toward the more basic challenges we experience on a daily basis.

In order to have that level of self-mastery, some people may believe they have to leave the material world behind and become for example, monks or nuns. That may be effective for some however, true self-mastery is not necessarily about giving up material things, but rather enjoying them without clinging to them or obsessing over them. It's all about embracing each moment of life with presence of mind, attentiveness and with a joyful spirit whatever your lifestyle looks like.

Here's a simple example of how we can get overly attached: John Smith falls in love with Jane Doe. He has never ever felt such a deep feeling of love in his life. Unfortunately, John Smith has some unresolved insecurities from his past and his sense of self-worth is somewhat low. He then associates the feeling he has of being in love with Jane as being the key to his freedom and fulfillment in life. Then, rather than integrating that love into his own well balanced life, he may begin to obsess on that wonderful feeling he has being around her; not realizing that the love he is experiencing for her actually lives within himself all the the time.

He just doesn't know it yet! So his so called love for Jane Doe soon turns to fear because by objectifying the love experience onto her, he then begins to fear losing her and may attempt to control her due to his strong feelings of jealousy. All he is really doing is pushing her away, the very thing he fears the most. I think you get the picture.

In the end, it is always about moderation and balance and basically being aware that the quality of all our relationships begin from within. That will ensure that we don't needlessly suffer and will be much more likely to get what we really want out of life.

So how do we practice self mastery?

The first step is to become aware of when we are losing our focus, our center, our sense of fully living in the present. Most of us know when we are becoming immersed with emotional and psychological turbulence, as I'm referring here, to getting off track for more than a short period of time.

Once we have determined that we are off track and need to do something about it, the second step is to get fed up enough about being in the mental and emotional ditch. It is difficult to turn things around unless you engage the emotions. Feeling fed up is one of the most powerful precursors toward taking effective action in your life. It can be very healthy to get fed up in a constructive way and channel those emotions of anger into decisive and effective action. Emotions are simply energy that we can channel into negative or positive actions and communication.

The third step is to self-talk our way into a new mindset doing whatever affirmation exercises we have access to in order to get back into the "zone". The fourth step is to take an appropriate and effective action that will complete the process of getting ourselves back on track. For example, let's say you have procrastinated for days about washing the dishes that have piled up in the sink. The feelings of frustration begin to grow; probably anger toward yourself for being so lazy. Once you're aware of your emotional state, feel free to cultivate a state of *"fed-uppedness"* by forcefully telling your negative mind, *"Thank you for sharing, but I'm not really interested."* Then simply mentally commit to taking action right away by walking up the stairs and washing the damn dishes!

In review, the one thing we do know is that the challenges we all face in life are coming whether we like them or not. The question is will we allow ourselves to become the victims of the challenges or see them as gold nuggets of opportunity for finally taking control of ourselves and our lives.

The more you practice this form of self-mastery, the more you will truly feel empowered and feel the self-confidence and resolve to take your life to a whole new level.

Connect with Your Challenges - Overview

In this chapter you learned how to conquer some of the obstacles and challenges you face every day in both your personal and professional life. You also learned how to react less and respond more. You learned how to avoid being a victim of these challenges and respond like a true warrior. You learned how to pick yourself up quickly and get back into the present moment, and into your true inner power. By mastering this step to a great degree you then master yourself, which is the key to success in every area of your life.

The following are common questions we receive about *busting barriers*:

Q. *I am a single mother of three children and find it almost impossible to lead a balanced life. Can you suggest some solutions?*

A. I know women who have several children and are victims of their circumstances, and by contrast I know other women who have several children and are mastering their lives beautifully. The difference every time is what the women are doing with their attitude, their personal boundaries and creativity of action during their chaotic schedules. You come to realize that you have so much more to give others when you create those simple boundaries.

By living more and more in your "zen zone" you are much more likely to respond than react toward others and also, more likely to access creative ideas for solutions to your specific challenges. Whether you are in prison, afflicted with a disease or are a single mother with several children, you always have the choice to be a victim or a master of your circumstances. As they say, where there is a will there is a way. All it takes is to have a warrior like spirit and a willingness to take whatever action needs to be taken to live your life happily and successfully, with true mastery.

Q. *What do you think about taking medication to deal with things such as depression?*

A. I would never try to play doctor, but here is what I recommend to some of my clients who are battling some form of depression and resist the idea of taking medication. I recommend they use every natural method they can to overcome it, through such things as coaching, therapy, meditation or anything else that would enhance their personal development. If these methods do not prove successful, they might need some form of medication for a while as they continue their personal growth journey.

Sometimes medication can help to take the edge off the pain and give you the time to work on yourself with less anxiety. Once you get strong enough, along with your doctors guidance, you will be able to wean yourself off of the medication. I believe there are times that some of the chronic conditions we suffer from have impacted our nervous systems to such a degree that traditional medicine may be needed for a while to take the edge off. However, it is essential to combine taking medication with an ongoing commitment to personal growth to ensure that the medication does not become simply a crutch.

Q. *I can see how you can master the little things in life, but when it comes to, for example, a loved one dying or a battle with a serious disease, I can't really see how we can master ourselves in those situations. Are you sure it's possible?*

A. There are so many examples of heroes around the world who have been challenged with all types of physical afflictions and circumstances that most of us think would be impossible to live with, let alone be able to maintain and embrace with an amazing attitude. Most of us don't really know how well we would respond to such challenges, but at the end of the day, no matter how bad our circumstances may be, the only control we do have is what we do with our own minds, emotions and actions; in fact, all the more reason to more seriously commit to mastering ourselves in every area of our lives.

Q. *With all this talk about self-mastery and self-development, doesn't it sound somewhat selfish and self-centered? Shouldn't life be more about serving and helping others?*

A. There is a big difference between working on yourself for your own self centered needs, and working on yourself so that you can be a better YOU for others. This program is not meant to be a "me-me" type of program. It's very much about serving others as depicted in steps #8 and #9. However, the giving must come from a healthy functioning self, as opposed to a limited or dysfunctional self. If your technology gadgets are working at only a 30% level of efficiency, wouldn't that negatively impact your productivity? In the same way, if you procrastinate or lack motivation, vision or self-confidence, wouldn't that decrease the effectiveness of your day-to-day actions and communication with other people? This program is not about self-centeredness, but much more about caring and giving to others built on a solid foundation of self-acceptance and self-respect. Now you are ready for the more advanced level of inner fitness, a stage I call "Connect with Your Magnetism."

Step #7 Connect With Your Magnetism

"People who ask confidently get more than those who are hesitant and uncertain. When you've figured out what you want to ask for, do it with certainty, boldness and confidence."

—Jack Canfield
(Author of "Chicken Soup for the Soul" and others)

There is a big difference between working on yourself for your own self centered needs, and working on yourself so that you can be a better YOU for others. This program is not meant to be a "me-me" type of program. It's very much about serving others as depicted in steps #8 and #9. However, the giving must come from a healthy functioning self, as opposed to a limited or dysfunctional self. If your technology gadgets are working at only a 30% level of efficiency, wouldn't that negatively impact your productivity? In the same way, if you procrastinate or lack motivation, vision or self-confidence, wouldn't that decrease the effectiveness of your day-to-day actions and communication with other people? This program is not about self-centeredness, but much more about caring and giving to others built on a solid foundation of self-acceptance and self-respect. Now you are ready for the more advanced level of inner fitness, a stage I call "Connect with Your Magnetism."

Are you ready for the magic to begin?

Now that you are living to a great degree in the stage of self mastery it's time to enjoy the benefits of being in such a state of grace. The following are just some of the benefits you will enjoy:

1. **Contentment-** this will be a welcomed feeling, especially being exposed to the stressed out world we live in today. You will find that you feel more at peace within yourself; whatever circumstances you may find yourself in. For some of you, this state is so foreign, so different from what you are used to that it's easy to fall into the trap of thinking that there is something wrong. There is absolutely nothing wrong. In fact there is everything right about living your life with more inner peace, balance and harmony. Shouldn't that be the norm? You will feel happier and more grateful for everything you have.

2. **Synchronicity-** you will find that as you enjoy more inner peace in your life there are so many more synchronistic moments. The more contentment you begin to feel inside yourself, the more in harmony you will feel with the outside world. You'll notice more magical moments in your life, things like people phoning you or bumping into you not long after you thought about them. Or opportunities you have visualized coming to fruition in ways you could not even begin to imagine. Most people experience synchronicity once in a while, but in the "state of

grace" you experience this much more often. That's when life becomes truly magical.

3. **Intuition-** the rational mind is an important and valuable tool for us to have in our lives. After all, we need the rational mind to know where to drive to, decide what to eat, plan events and many other day to day tasks. But the intuitive mind taps into a whole new dimension of awareness. That's where we access deep inner wisdom that provides insights and revelations that border on the spiritual. For those of you who believe in a higher force, this is one way it can assist us in our lives more effectively. When you experience an intuition, it is more than a passing thought, it is a deep *knowing* that almost always leads us to make solid and accurate choices and decisions in our lives.

4. **Presence of Mind-** this is what is meant by the power of *now*. Most of us are living way too much in the past or the future, due most often to the emotional and psychological turbulences we spoke about earlier. By living in the *now*; in the present moment, we are able to free ourselves from pre-occupations with the past and future. Of course it's nice to reminisce at times about the past and fantasize or visualize the future, but many of us begin obsessing on these, and doing so, takes us away from truly embracing each moment fully. Last week I read an article about a recent study that indicates that goldfish, believe it or not, now have greater attention spans than human beings. How sad! They attribute much of that to our obsession with technology gadgets where our minds are constantly jumping to what's next, as opposed to simply enjoying and relishing each moment. We would all be wise to maintain some

sense of innocence within this ever changing world of technology.

5. **Listening-** another benefit of self mastery and living with more inner freedom and peace of mind is that you become a better listener. You not only develop more awareness of yourself, but also begin to master the art of listening within all of your relationships. Others will feel more trust and confidence toward you as they see how attentive you are when listening to them. They will also appreciate the level of interest you take through the quality and sincerity of your follow up questions. People will think, "Hey this person really listens and really cares'" The art of active listening also means you will be very aware of who you are speaking with and how to respond to them most effectively. You cannot imagine the benefits you will experience in all of your relationships by mastering your questioning and listening skills.

6. **Managing Stress-** by living in the "zone" most of the time you will also benefit by significantly minimizing your stress levels. Stress is most often triggered by conditions outside ourselves, be it relationships, financial or political. The reality is that stress does not really come from any of these, but in fact, from what we do internally with our own thoughts and feelings about them. As we master ourselves, we find that very little in life can get us off track for long. I have a strong feeling this is what the Eastern Masters call a state of 'enlightenment'.

7. **Turbo Charged Inner Fitness-** another benefit of living in this state is that you can take all the inner fitness techniques in step #4 to a whole next level. Now you are truly ready to ascend the inner Mount

Everest. We know that the mind and emotions play a vital role in creating the life we want. We learned that in step 4.

I highly recommend taking 10 to 15 minutes in the morning to do your inner fitness exercises. That's easy enough, but what about the other 23 hours and 45 minutes? The key here is to sustain the focus of self mastery on a continual basis. When I say continual, I don't mean that you consciously focus on it all day. I mean that when you have some time to reflect, instead of allowing negativity and doubt to creep into your consciousness, choose rather to focus on feeling what you would like to attract into your life, as if it were actually with you right now. It goes beyond repeating an affirmation but rather feeling it at a depth level. Now that you are living more and more in a state of grace, your goal should be to sustain those feelings as much as possible on an ongoing basis.

Imagine for a second that you had the freedom to do whatever you wanted to and experience whatever you wished to experience. How would you actually *feel* if that were so? Maybe the feelings would include peace, relief, excitement, freedom or passion. Take a moment to actually feel those feelings now. As you feel them, you will likely say *"WOW, yes, that feels great! It is as if it's right here right now, I am so grateful."* The point here is to focus more on your feelings than on your thoughts. It might sound a little frivolous but remember the heart and emotions are the most powerful part of manifesting what you want, and you need to build and continually strengthen those inner muscles. It will initially take discipline and patience but if you persevere, you will be amazed at the results as you see yourself beginning to live the extraordinary life you always dreamed about. That's true magnetism!

The trick is to maintain those feelings as often as possible every day. It can be about health, relationships, prosperity or whatever you choose. Simply express silently and with strong inner emotional conviction how amazing it feels to already have it. This exercise combines gratefulness with the cultivation of your ability to receive. The more intensively and repeatedly you maintain these *feeling* states, the faster and stronger your goals will be realized. Obviously all this inner work needs to be followed up with appropriate and effective actions. But keep in mind that as you master your inner world, you have much greater access to your intuitive mind, which in many ways will guide you to act appropriately and effectively.

Please remember that not all of your goals will be achieved right away. Some will, but others will take time. That's where patience, belief and enjoying the process kick in. If you practice this simple routine consistently and resist all tendencies to regress into self-doubt, you will notice that great things will happen faster than you think. Keep in mind, that your goals need not be huge ones. Living an extraordinary life does not necessarily mean being a millionaire, unless that is one of your goals. What is important here is you being clear on what you want your life to look like and then commit to that vision. It could be as simple as working in finance, being a carpenter or be a very successful business person or entrepreneur. Don't get caught up in what others expect you to achieve, rather, always be true to YOU!

The Power of Unconditional Love

When it comes to attracting what we want, at times we can get a little selfish by focusing too much on our own personal needs. The irony is that the highest levels of success come to us, less by what we attract, and more by how joyfully and compassionately we live our lives and radiate that outward. Quite often we gain a lot more satisfaction by giving than receiving. When I first took up the practice of meditation, all I cared about was to achieve some freedom and relief from my hyperactive mind.

With continued practice I experienced more and more calmness and mental concentration. Then something shifted; beneath all the calmness and peace was a strong feeling of compassion that began to well up in me. I just wanted to share the benefits of what I was experiencing with others. I began to realize that personal development was a much deeper experience *if* it included a higher meaning and purpose than simply seeking our own happiness. I came to see that for example a nice car or the latest technology gadget might make me happy in the moment, but loving and helping others would produce a much greater and long lasting sense of inner joy.

Up until this point, this 9-step program has focused on the importance of having a great relationship with yourself. Not because you're selfish or self centered, but rather because you were responsible enough to lay the groundwork for successful relationships with others and with the world around you. That is why at this stage in the process it is time to extend the benefits of working on yourself into all of your personal and professional relationships. Have you ever noticed as you walk down the street that you find yourself being overly critical and judgmental toward the people you see? I can certainly relate to that. There was a time in my life when I noticed how critical and judgmental I was of people, especially when people watching. In order to turn that pattern around I began doing a simple exercise. As I passed each person I silently wished them WELL. I would repeat over and over again, "I *wish you well Sir, I wish you well Miss, "* and continued doing this for an hour or so.

To my astonishment, within a very short period of time I began to feel more peaceful, accepting and loving toward everyone around me. Could you imagine how life would be if each of us cultivated a little more compassion. Our human relationships are like a workshop for us to learn the art of loving.

And yet, I truly believe that the main reason that some people fall in and out of love so quickly is that they never really learn how to genuinely adore and love the other person unconditionally. Rather, it becomes more about what the other person does for me. It becomes more about "what am I getting out of the relationship" than "what am I bringing to the table", especially in the form of loving them exactly for who they are.

So one simple exercise you can do during your normal day is to silently wish people around you well and send them positive thoughts and feelings. Commit to communicate with love and compassion with each person you speak with. In general, make a decision to care about every person you encounter, even if you observe things about them you do not like. We don't have to like everyone, but we can have compassion for everyone.

If you begin to make this a daily practice, you'll be amazed at not only what comes back to you, but at the freedom and joy you will feel. The vibes you put out will be electromagnetic and people around you will feel them whether you know it or not. Did you ever notice, that very little good comes to you when you are in an angry or sad state? But as soon as you project good thoughts and feelings, things tend to flow more freely and you begin to experience *harmony* in all of your relationships with others.

Many of us are blocking this flow through emotional guardedness, control, manipulation, and pretentiousness, all of which leaves us the feeling of being isolated, alone and disconnected from others. If you truly want to attract and connect with great people into your life, then maybe it's time to let the guard down and commit to cultivating compassion for others.

Being compassionate does not mean being happy all the time. Sometimes a person might need *tough love* from you, because being someone who genuinely cares is not about being a doormat or an enabler. There are times when loving unconditionally means that you care enough to be honest and direct, and however painful it may be for the other person to hear, in the end it could be the very thing that will make a difference in that persons life. I can promise you that if you make a determined effort to love unconditionally day after day, the benefits that will come your way will astonish you.

Connect with Your Magnetism- Overview

In this chapter you learned how to take the basic inner fitness exercises that you learned in step #4 to a whole new level. You learned how step # 7 is all about enjoying the fruits of your labor. You learned about all the benefits of truly surrendering and letting go of the more subtle mental and emotional turbulence, and about the importance and power of unconditional love.

The following are common questions we receive about Connect with Your Magnetism:

Q. *I thought I was at this stage already but now I see that I am not. How do I get there?*

A. Many of us think we are, but quite often is in fact no more than an intellectual understanding. For example, you may know intellectually that you would like to meet the person of your dreams. But as you look deeper into yourself you might discover that your true conviction around deserving that type of relationship may not be in alignment with your intellectual understanding of it. It is essential for us to tap into that deep conviction in order to experience more grace, magnetism and synchronicity.

Q. *How do I do that specifically?*

A. The first thing is identify the reason your belief is not strong. If it's due to old patterns that still haunt you, you may have to return to step #4 to reinforce the re-programming process. This time you might choose to be more specific about the issue at hand. I also mentioned that these stages are fluid. Reaching a stage does not mean you never fall back, it just means that you hang out in one stage or another until you master it. At times you may have to return to previous stages in order to deal with new and immediate challenges in your life and then make your way back up the ladder to the higher stages. If the reason was not due to past issues then you may simply need to strengthen step #7, which is all about practicing with more intensity your more advanced motivational techniques.

Q. *After all my work on personal development, the reality is that I am still not achieving my goals in life. Why am I not achieving them? Sometimes I think all this motivational jargon is way too simplistic.*

A. You are not alone. Most people who commit to some sort of "inner work" feel the same way at times. Please remember that this is not for the faint of heart. It takes a lot of courage, faith and determination to succeed. The key is to never give up, and most importantly to make sure that you are working on all nine stages discussed in this book.

We have now completed steps 1 through 7 which are all about the commitment YOU have to yourself. It's all about learning to accept, adore, love and respect yourself like you would your own child. Now we are ready to focus our attention on the communication we have with others. As I have said before, about 80% of our communication with others depends on the first 7 steps. When we are truly content, motivated, and living life with self mastery and compassion, the resulting joy that exudes from us will have more impact on others than anything else could. The other 20% has more do with the words we speak, it's about content and technique. By combining your personal development with your communication mastery, you truly become an irresistible force in the world.

Step # 8 Connect With Others

"We have two ears and one mouth so that we can listen twice as much as we speak."

—*Epictetus, Greek philosopher*

"Communication works for those who work at it."

—*John Powell*

Now that you are living at a much higher level of self-mastery and personal power you will find that life becomes simpler, more fun and much more productive. You are now able to focus on refining and perfecting your communication skills at a whole new level. Self-mastery is the key to successful relationships because we bring all of who we are into each communication with each person we connect with, and into every relationship we have. In a sense, we were born into an arranged marriage with ourselves; we literally spend 24/7 with the person we see every day in the mirror. Pretty amazing, isn't it? The more we cherish and cultivate that primary relationship with ourselves, the more success we will achieve in every other relationship we have, both personally and professionally

Thinking about that for a second, it becomes much clearer why there are so many dysfunctional relationships in the world. How can we possibly respect and love others the way we would like, if we continue to be so critical and hard on ourselves? The anger, frustration and fear will inevitably *oooze* out into all of the relationships we have and unfortunately, for the most part toward the ones we are closest to and love the most. So if we are to have great relationships with other people, we better cultivate a pretty amazing relationship with ourselves first.

Let's clarify what it is we mean by the word "communication". We have all learned over the years that a very small percent of successful communication comes from the actual content or words you speak. A much larger percent has to do with the more intangible qualities such as tone of voice, clarity of speech, self-confidence, patience, passion, listening skills and self-awareness.

All of these have to do with the quality of the relationship we have with ourselves, which we covered in the previous chapters. Now we will turn our attention to the content and technique part of communication. In this section, I will cover what I consider to be a few of the more important categories on the subject and provide tools and techniques you can use right away to enhance your own communication with others.

BREAKING THE ICE

Whether you are in sales or simply attempting to meet someone in a social setting, it is always important to make a good first impression. Unfortunately, many of us allow fear and insecurity to limit our ability to connect effectively with others; often projecting ourselves as less than we actually are. Some people are overly timid or shy and have trouble asserting themselves. while others on the opposite extreme can be overly aggressive and pushy trying way too hard to control or impress others. Most people will consciously or unconsciously pick up on these patterns, and be on guard. To truly make a first great impression, nothing is more important than being genuine, down-to-earth and authentic. It is essential to create an environment that allows the person you are with to feel comfortable and relaxed enough to be themselves in your presence. That will make it much easier for them to trust you, have more confidence in you and be much more receptive to know you better.

I have learned a lot from some pretty amazing mentors over the years. Some in the areas of business, others in the areas of personal development and spirituality, but the one who helped me most to learn how to relax and have fun is an unlikely source. His name was Dean Martin, a member of the Rat Pack with Frank Sinatra in the 1960s. In my opinion, Dean Martin was one of the greatest personalities of all time. He was a good singer, but his personality was what made him so unique. Oh yes, he had the image of being a drinker, but most of that was part of the fad of his era—he was actually drinking apple juice on stage.

If you look behind his image, you see an amazing person who projected an energy that impacted millions of people around the world for decades. In fact, he had the #1 rated variety show for almost a decade watched by over 50,000,000 people around the world. People simply adored him, mainly because he had the ability to make you smile. That's the power of the heart! Earlier we referred to the area of relationships and how the human heart is much more powerful in influencing others than the human brain. Dean Martin had very little formal education, but very few people had the charm, spontaneity and joyful spirit he had.

To this day I still send a few of his YouTube clips to some of my more serious clients to help lighten them up. If you are able to make people smile or laugh, you are well on your way to attracting more friends, inspiring others at work and generally having more impact in all your relationships. I call it the "Dean Martin principle".

By being authentic you create the conditions for people to trust you and feel more comfortable around you. If on the other hand, they sense too much "guardedness" or control, naturally they will back off. Whatever the situation, by simply being yourself people are much more likely to endear themselves to you. That is why breaking the ice effectively is such a important first step toward cultivating successful relationships.

QUESTIONING SKILLS

Connecting effectively with others, however important this may be, is only the first step. After having connected successfully, some of us may then fall into the trap of talking way too much about ourselves or the opposite, not talking enough. The goal is to find a healthy balance between questioning and listening. The more aware and knowledgeable we are about the the person we're with at the time, the greater is our ability to maximize the quality and effectiveness of our responses.

To accomplish this, it's vitally important to be mindfully present when the other person is speaking, not only to really hear what they say, but also to tune into the more subtle non-verbal language such as eye contact, facial expressions and gestures. Often these tell us more than the words do. It's also important to master the art of asking creative, thoughtful and interesting questions. Of course part of the assessment will be picking up on non-verbal language as well, but in most cases when we first meet someone, conversation is a big part of the interaction, and it is important that we to do it well.

When it comes to romance, how many of you remember meeting someone really HOT, but within ten minutes or so, found that same person to be quite unattractive to you? They were either too self-centered or perhaps just plain boring. For example, many men don't realize how important the role the mind and personality play in attracting a mate. Sorry guys, muscle building alone may not be enough.

Some men actually think that if they flex their muscles or wallets, they will be the "ultimate chick magnet". Sorry Bob, although these qualities may help your overall attractiveness, most quality women will ultimately not be impressed by those qualities alone. It's amazing how often I have heard women friends say to me that it is actually the mind and personality of a man that is the true aphrodisiac.

Many single people today are using the Internet to meet. Whatever we think of this vehicle for meeting others, it does require some effective communication skills in order to be successful at it. It means making an effort expressing yourself in a way that will pique the other person's interest, and people love it when you also ask intelligent and creative questions.

The following is a simple example of how to communicate effectively with someone over the Internet, such as you would if you were instant messaging on a dating site:

YOU: Hi there.

THEY: Hi.

YOU: I'm Bob, by the way. Are you from New York originally?

THEY: I'm Maria, and yes, all my life. How about yourself?

YOU: I'm from San Diego. I've heard so many great things about New York, but never actually been there.

THEY: You can't be serious! Well you must visit sometime.

YOU: Well if we get along, who knows? LOL. How has this site been? Is it tough meeting a quality guy?

THEY: It's been OK. Some weirdos and a few nice men, but I haven't met anyone I have really connected with yet. Yes, it can be challenging these days.

YOU: I hear that a lot. I take pride in the fact that I really respect women and am looking for a genuine and serious relationship.

THEY: That is so refreshing.

And off you go. This type of questioning and answering is a great way to connect and create rapport in order to assure the other person they are connecting with a quality person worthy of connecting with again. Did you notice that in this example, it's not just about asking a question for the sake of asking a question, and then quickly returning to talking about yourself? Dig a little and show some genuine interest by asking follow up questions. It will make the other person feel that you are genuinely curious about them and will give them confidence that your life is not just about you and your own needs. Remember, we all want to be respected and loved. If you strengthen this skill, you will be amazed at how many people will comment on how good a listener and communicator you are. People will be drawn to you and this will make it easier for you to go the next level of cultivating a relationship with them.

LISTENING SKILLS

Ah, the listening skills! Many people struggle with this one for a variety of reasons. One reason may be due to self-centeredness and narcissism. This personality type doesn't much care about what the other person says, because they are so overly obsessed with themselves. Another reason for poor listening skills could be due to the person having a hyperactive mind. These people have trouble focusing on listening because they are so busy thinking about what they will say next, or about something else completely as their minds gets so easily distracted. Very few of us have the discipline and presence of mind to give our undivided attention while listening to others.

As a result, many social connections we have with people tend to be on a relatively superficial level. You may not care, especially if the attraction is primarily physical, but most often people do want more. Rather than using effective questioning and listening skills in order to deepen and enrich the communication, the back and forth chit chat often only touches the surface. It then descends into a lower level interaction, something a good friend of mine calls "barking and meowing."

A conversation that lacks humor and depth quickly becomes boring especially for quality people who expect more from a communication. So what can we do? Well, here is a simple yet effective exercise you can use to strengthen your listening muscles. First, find a willing partner.

You begin by asking them any question, not one that only require a simple yes or no answer, but rather a response of at least two or three sentences. For example, *'what are the main reasons you moved from New York to LA?* When they are finished answering, your task is to repeat to them what they just said, not necessarily word for word, but should include the major points they communicated to you. When you finish your part of the communication, your partner decides if you have repeated the main points accurately, and if not, you get to repeat what you said for a second time. They continue to do this until you get it right. Then, if you have time, you move on to another question. You may find this exercise to be somewhat frustrating initially because you are working so hard to focus on what they are saying, but once you begin mastering it, watch the effect it has on all of your business and personal communications

Effective listening will help you gain the trust of others very quickly, so long as it is not forced. It must be genuine. That means really listening and hearing what and how the other person is communicating. Remember, you are not doing this to prove that you are nice. You are doing this, first and foremost, to respect the person you are with, listening to what they have to say and to have a better idea of how to respond appropriately and effectively to what they are saying.

There is a big difference between what we call passive listening and active listening. When you listen passively, you might half heartedly listen but without really responding and engaging in any real way. Active listening on the other hand, really connects you with the person. You are more pro-actively participating in the conversation with your objections, questions or comments.

PERSONALITY TYPES

The following are some examples of different types of people you will encounter and how to effectively respond to them.

1. Mr./Ms. **Timid and Shy:** These people are especially fearful and cautious. If you do not wish to scare them away, you might choose to be more sensitive and compassionate in your communication approach to them. When you go into a crying baby's room, you would likely sing a lullaby to soothe them, not play rap music.

2. Mr/Ms **Macho:** These people usually have big egos and liked to be looked up to. But they generally don't respect weakness. So you may want to appeal to their egos by complimenting them but also by being assertive in order to gain their respect.

3. Mr. /Ms **Scatter Brained:** These people often have trouble staying focused and on topic. You may need to jump into the conversation from time to time to help keep the conversation on track. This is an example of where your active listening skills need to kick in, as the other person cannot be trusted to keep things focused and on task.

4. Mr. /Ms **Sad and Lonely:** This is when you have to play "psychologist." focusing less on what you want to say, and more on drawing them out of themselves. This might mean allowing them to clear the air and get things off their chest. Feeling somewhat relieved, they will more likely be in a receptive state to listen to what you actually have to say and the interaction will become a more quality two-way communication.

5. Mr. /Ms **Skeptical:** Some people are very practical and detailed-oriented. You might have to back up some of the things you speak about with factual truths and information. This will help convince them because they do not normally relate to emotion or hype of any kind.

PRESENTATION SKILLS

More and more people today are taking charge of their own financial lives by becoming entrepreneurs. There are more people today in small business and home-based businesses than ever before. Many have chosen this path because of a deep-seated desire to fulfill their career passion, while others have chosen this path out of necessity, perhaps due to a shaky economy. Whatever the reasons, the important question to ask is, what can we do to ensure success as an entrepreneur today?

Well, I am sure there are many factors, but for the purposes of this program, I would like to highlight those that pertain to interpersonal communication. The truth is that in order to be successful today, highly effective relationship building skills, both online and off-line are essential. Since I am not an expert in Internet marketing and social media I will not say too much about that subject here. However, I do know enough to understand that even online, relationship building skills are crucial to success. I will focus here instead on the more practical human skills we need to have while networking, phoning and presentation skills.

NETWORKING

I don't think anyone would argue that we live in an era where networking is of utmost importance, in both social online networking and in "belly to belly" live connections with others. Never has it been more important to effectively connect with others and cultivate relationships for the purpose of promoting our products, services or projects. And that means getting out there and being visible. Most of us don't schedule networking activities like we would schedule say, our fitness activities. The following are a few key reminders for you to keep in mind as you master the art of networking:

1. LISTS: Make a list of all the meetings, trade shows and events that you feel you need to attend over the next few months and mark them on your calendar.

2. PROMO MATERIALS: Make sure that you have all the necessary promotional materials that are appropriate for the occasion.

3. DISCIPLINE: Make sure that you commit to meeting as many quality and targeted contacts as possible while you are at an event to ensure that you made the best use of your time.

4. WORKING THE ROOM: Make sure that you do not allow yourself to get into a comfort zone by spending too much time with people you already know. It is very easy to slacken while networking by taking the easy way out and communicating with people you already know.

5. URGENCY: Remember you have a short window of time to meet as many quality people as you can. Create a goal of how many people you would like to meet at that event and then take action to ensure you achieve that goal. For example, if you are attending a trade show you may have a goal to gather at least 50 business cards before you leave the event that day. Or, your goal might be meeting 5

quality people, as the goal is not about the number of people you meet, but more about the right people. If you approach each networking event in this way, you will always go home feeling a greater sense of accomplishment and can then look forward to following up on all your warm leads.

6. BREAKING THE ICE: Make sure that you connect with each person you meet in a very down-to-earth and genuine way. Even though your goal may be to secure business or receive a referral, it is important to first connect initially in a very warm and human way. Doing this will more likely open the door for more interactions with that person.

7. EXPECTATIONS: It is important that you do not have unrealistic expectations of how each person will react or respond to you. Be focused less on the result and more on the process of connecting effectively. The thing you can control is the impression you make *and leave* on that person. If you focus on being relaxed and genuine, you can be assured that good things will flow from that.

8. FOLLOW-UP: Many people wrongly expect that by just getting out there and networking, business will automatically come their way. In reality, it is rarely that simple. Building your business is much like developing a personal relationship. It usually takes time, and will require patience, determination and a strong willingness to take whatever steps you need to in order to make it happen. Part of that includes following up on the connections you do make. So instead of throwing business cards out or filing them away for years, I suggest you schedule time each day to follow up with each and every person. This will give you the opportunity to do business

with them, set up a joint venture or at the very least, agree to stay in touch.

9. SELECTIVE NETWORKING: For some of you it is more about the quality and not the quantity of leads. If you are just starting out in business or have a product or service that has broad appeal, then focusing on meeting as many people as possible may be an effective strategy. However, if you have a very targeted or exclusive audience, say high net worth individuals, your networking may require a more focused strategy. Either way effective communication is always the key!

MARKETING STRATEGIES

You can have all the talent and skill in the world. You may have an amazing personality and be an effective communicator, but at the end of the day, you need to maximize your ability to attract more clients to you. There are many marketing strategies you can choose from so I'm simply recommending here that you access experts in the appropriate field to help you understand your target audience, and how best to make an impression on them.

You may need a branding expert, a business coach or social media management company. What you have learned so far in this book is mostly about your mindset, self-confidence and your ability to strengthen all of your relationships and communication with others. If you are an entrepreneur it will also be essential that you add into the mix highly targeted marketing strategies to effectively build your business.

TELEPHONE SKILLS

Ah, the telephone. The thought of doing cold calls sends shivers up the spines of most entrepreneurs. The reality is that we cannot escape from using of the phone. We may not need to do cold calls but we do need to make calls, period. I don't care whether they are cold, warm, hot or lukewarm; the fact is that we generally need at some point to connect with others over the phone, and so it is important that we do it effectively.

When it comes to initial contact over the phone I have seen two patterns of behavior. One leans too far to the side of a "canned" presentation, which of course turns most people off, because it's overly scripted, salesy and monotonous. On the other hand, there are people who improvise, wing-it or "adlib" their communication. As they 'hem and haw' their way through the presentation, the lack of cohesiveness and structure often causes the listener to loses interest and respect. The solution is to have what I call a planned and personalized presentation. It begins with creating a script that has all the necessary points you wish to communicate. Once memorized, the script can be personalized according to your own style and personality. The following points are the key ingredients you may want to have in each call:

Grounding Statement:

"Good morning, Mr. /Mrs. Jones. This is _____calling. I happened to pick your business card up at _____ trade show last week, and thought that I would give you a call. By the way, how did you enjoy the show?"

By using this type of grounding statement, you connect with the person without sounding too much like a salesperson. They also have a clearer idea of where they might have met you, making them less guarded and more comfortable about the call. Some other examples of grounding statements may be:

"Good *afternoon, Mr. /Mrs. ____.This is_____ calling. I happened to see the name of your company listed in the ____ directory, and I thought I would give you a call."*

"Good *afternoon, Mr. /Mrs.   . I happened to be speaking to a good friend of yours yesterday _____ and they recommended I give you a call. By the way, how do you know _____?"*

Power Benefit Statements:

Once you have made the initial contact, you have a short window of time to pique their interest and get their attention. Many people make the mistake of talking about what they do instead of about how you can help them. Check out the difference in the following example of a financial advisor who is making an initial call with the goal of getting an appointment.

"Hello *Mr. /Mrs. ____. My name is ___ calling from ___. We provide a number of financial services including blah, blah, blah and blah. I would like to know if we can set up an appointment so that I can show you in more detail how I can help you."*

Ouch. Out of ten calls, how many people do you think would say *yes?*

Here's a better option:

"Hello, Mr. /Mrs. ___. This is   calling from   .I happened to see your name listed in the Board of Trade directory and I thought I would give you a call.(chit chat as much as is appropriate) I am currently providing my clients in the_____ area with some very important financial information. Many of them had no idea that the government is now providing $7,200 per child to secure their long-term education. Were you aware of that? (NO) Would you be interested in receiving more information on this? GREAT, What I am doing is setting up very brief meetings over the next two weeks to explain in more detail exactly how this program can be of help to you and your family."

By approaching it this way, you are being more practical about your offer and are communicating in a more down to earth way about how you can help them. You're also using language that will have stronger *emotional* impact on them, a proven method that will absolutely increase the productivity of your phone calls.

Questions:

There are times that a qualifying question or two might be in order, such as the following:

"If you were interested in our program, would $2,000 be an investment that you could make at this time? " "Do you currently have any   ?"

Closing:

Now we are ready to bring the conversation to a close. The following is a soft but effective way to do it:

"I am setting up very brief appointments in the ___ area over the next two weeks just to go over in more detail exactly how this program can be of help to you and your family. "

If they say *"OK,"* you can say, *"Well, according to my schedule, I have ___ or ___afternoon free. Which one works best for you?"*

They respond, and then you reply with, *"Great, how about ___ pm?"* If they say *"neither, "* you can say, *"Which day in the next week works for you?"* If they respond with *—Thursday, "* you confirm, *" Great, how about 1:00pm?"* And if they are still not sure they feel comfortable setting up an appointment, you can always provide them with more information via email.

By making a phone call in this way, it will provide you an opportunity within a short window of time to build some rapport, focus on benefits *for them,* and in general, sound more human and less like a fast-talking salesperson.

SOCIAL MEDIA

Although I would never call myself an expert in social media, I do know enough about it to understand its power and importance. Like anything else, it requires moderation. On one extreme we have people who have become obsessed with it, even to the point of losing the effectiveness of their day to day human interaction skills. On the other extreme (especially the older crowd) we have those who tend to reject social media outright. Of course, most of us know that if you are in business today, you have to keep up with the times. Building your business usually means creating and establishing long lasting relationships, and today that also means using online strategies to connect effectively with others.

The reality is that many of the same qualities we need to strengthen our day to day communications with others hold true for online communication as well. It is important to listen, to ask good questions, to engage people and to share ideas and information. If used effectively social media can be a very powerful vehicle to attract, connect and impact others. It is definitely not something to be dismissed, but rather embraced as an enhancement tool for our communications with other people.

Connect with Others- Overview

In this chapter you learned to communicate with more impact in your professional and personal relationships. You learned about the importance of developing and strengthening your questioning and listening skills. You also learned the importance of being aware of the different personality types and how to effectively respond to each one. You also learned some key points related to marketing a product or service within a relationship building process.

The following are common questions we receive about *transforming business and personal relationships*:

Q. *Why do I keep attracting the wrong kind of men into my life?*

A.   There are two main reasons why that might be happening. The first is that you might be one of those trusting souls who makes impulsive decisions before really getting to know someone. So you meet someone who is attractive enough and seems nice but without doing proper due diligence, you may in time begin to see the cracks in the armor and wonder why. We have certainly lost the art of courtship in this fast paced world.

The other reason may have to do more with who you are, meaning where you are in your own personal development and in your life. Remember the energy we project outward into the world usually comes right back to us. So if we have unresolved personal issues, we are more likely to find a mate who has those as well. Or, we might just be the caregiver type who gives too much and keeps attracting a growing number of co-dependent relationships.

Q. *How do we teach our children to be grateful?*

A. I believe we teach most effectively by being an example of what we teach. Instruction, words and reminders of course help, however, if you teach by example you will likely have much more impact in teaching your children than any preaching will ever do. Children need instruction and wisdom which may include a dose of tough love at times. They may not appreciate it immediately, but over a period of time, perhaps when they are living on their own, they are more likely to feel grateful for what you taught them over the years.

Q. *Recently, my wife began complaining about my family. She doesn't like the way they disrespect me and she has become preoccupied with it. I don't really think my family will ever change and I don't let it bother me, but my wife's negativity is beginning to get to me.*

A. The fact that your wife cares about how you are being treated by your family is commendable. So, I recommend that you first have a heart to heart with your family asserting clearly how you and your wife feel. If that does not work, perhaps spend less time with them so they begin to see that you are not willing to accept their behavior.

Regarding your wife being preoccupied with your family's attitudes, you may try to encourage her not to let that ruin the joy of your life together. Try to get her to lighten up a bit because if the negativity in your household persists, then both of you will be the victims, and at that point it won't really have anything to do with your family, but more about how you both respond to the challenges of having to deal with your difficult family.

Q. *My boyfriend and I are having a lot of problems. I keep attracting dysfunctional relationships. How do I change that?*

A. Attracting less than desirable relationships can be a result of one of two things. The first has to do with not taking enough time to get to know someone. We live in a very fast world that expects quick results, and when it comes to personal relationships, it just doesn't work that way. For heaven's sake, take your time. The second and more common reason for attracting dysfunctional relationships is that we may in fact have a dysfunctional relationship with ourselves, and so like attracts like. If you want to ensure that you draw in higher quality relationships, then, as I have said throughout this book, you may want to raise the bar with the relationship you have with yourself. By doing this, you will likely have a much clearer picture of the kinds of qualities that you really want and expect from a relationship with others.

Q. *Sometimes I feel like my girlfriend and I are so compatible and at other times I feel like we are so different. Is this relationship right for me?*

A. It's not so much if the relationship is right or not. It is more about whether the relationship is a functional and uplifting relationship or a codependent and dysfunctional one.

Here is a simple exercise you can do to see if this relationship is worth preserving. Go ahead and rate the relationship in the following categories with a score of 1-10 (1 is low, 10 is high): physical attraction, mental compatibility, sense of humor and laughter, values, lifestyle goals, spiritual beliefs, ambition, financial success. If you see several low scores in some key categories, you may ask yourself the following question: "Why am I willing to accept so much less than what I desire and deserve?"

Perhaps by doing such an exercise you may get your answer or at least become clearer on the quality of relationship you do have. If you are still committed to saving the relationship, you can talk with your partner about how to shore up the weak links. Failing that, you can choose to move on with your life, committed to doing whatever it takes to heal and learn from your mistakes, and ultimately look forward to attracting a more fulfilling relationship.

Q. *How do you motivate others to see what is so obvious to you?*

A. You cannot really motivate others to see what you see. All you can do is express your views and then it is up to the other person to understand and perhaps embrace your view. You cannot really force your ideas on others because that's not your responsibility. The nature of your question almost implies that you want to change someone to agree with what you see, and part of the problem may lie in your own unrealistic expectation to change them. If you drop the expectation, and simply communicate as best you can, you will be more at peace with yourself whether they agree with you or not.

Q. *How can you be a true friend to someone whose opinions about life are often so different from yours?*

A. Being a true friend doesn't necessarily have anything to do with having the same opinions. As a matter of fact, having different opinions might be an enriching experience, as you both can enjoy being exposed to other viewpoints. Being a great friend is more about trust, honesty and open and effective communication, irrespective of what your opinions may be. If on the other hand there is so little in common between you and this person, and you are simply with them out of guilt or filling up space in your life, then you may choose to end the relationship.

Step #9 Connect With The World

"The world is not interested in what we do for a living. What they are interested in is what we have to offer freely - hope, strength, love and the power to make a difference!"

—Sasha Azevedo

With the foundation of a strong mindset and ever improving communication skills, you should be living your life with more inner peace, happiness and success. It's interesting to note that the more joy and fulfillment we feel in our own lives, the greater our inclination to give back to society. The reality is that when our lives are filled with confusion or too much stress, it is more difficult to feel a deep sense of compassion toward others. During those times we tend to focus more on ourselves and on our own survival as we continue discovering our way in this world. That is normal and expected, but once you begin to experience a degree of success and fulfillment in your life, you will more than likely be attracted to making an impact on others, and ultimately leaving some sort of personal legacy.

Making an impact does not necessarily mean getting involved in some big picture project like saving starving children in some far off land. For some, it might simply be about making a difference in a local school system or getting involved with Big Brothers or Sisters. It could be local or global, whatever calls to you.

If you are not sure how or where to give back, you can try a simple brainstorming exercise. Write down almost every possible social interest category that you can imagine. It could include mental health, environment, politics, homelessness, youth, health and wellness; whatever interests you. Rate your passion for each category by giving it a mark from 1 to 10. By doing this exercise, you will get closer to the one that means the most to you. If you've chosen the area of health, then you can repeat the very same exercise with sub-categories related to health, and by the end of that exercise you will have more clarity, for example, working specifically in long-term care for the elderly.

Helping others comes from having a spirit of gratefulness for your own life wherein you begin to experience a desire to give back to others who may not be as fortunate, or to those who are in need of your support, mentorship or guidance.

HOW WILL YOU MAKE AN IMPACT?

I recommend you take a piece of paper and write out "How Will I Make An Impact?" at the top of the page. Beneath the title, name the project that you most wish to focus on and describe it in at least one or two paragraphs, taking as much time as you need.

Now that you have confirmed your vision and commitment in that area, you will realize you cannot accomplish this alone. That is why it can be very useful to create a Legacy Circle consisting of 6 people who will support each other to make an impact in the world. Given that we can only accomplish so much on our own, we often need to look at external resources to help support our dreams and visions. In the corporate world, a senior manager need only make a simple call and is able to set up a team meeting of trusted advisors. Most people don't have that same luxury, and therefore need to be somewhat creative in setting up such support systems for becoming Legacy Leaders. There is growing unrest today, especially among young people, many of whom sense that there is something wrong with our existing corporate and financial institutions. And so, it becomes more important than ever to go beyond attitudes of protest and blame, by choosing a more pro-active approach to create positive change in the world. Legacy Circles can be a very powerful tool to help create this change.

So on your project page you can begin by listing five or six people you admire and trust the most, to help support you in making an impact. Select people who would likely share your desire to make a difference in the world.

Setting up Legacy Circles again is a simple and powerful way to achieve your goals. Each group is made up of like-minded individuals who often have complimentary talents and skills that make for a highly effective support system. The first thing to do in setting up such a group is to clearly know what your needs are in terms of expertise. You may choose an internet marketing person, an accountant, an event planner, financial advisor and perhaps a lawyer or a PR person.

You then connect with people you know in those industries who you would enjoy working with and who would likely connect well with the others that you plan to invite. If you don't know someone personally in an area of need, you can either look for them through others in the group or through further networking efforts. Once you have the group in place, set up the first meeting. In your initial contact with each person you can explain that you are thinking of creating Legacy Groups consisting of like-minded individuals for the purpose of helping and supporting each other toward making an impact in the world.

The first meeting would be for the purpose of building rapport, and for you as the leader to have an opportunity to articulate the vision and purpose of the group concept. One of the goals of the first meeting would be to garner commitments in doing these meetings on a regular basis, for a period of time that you agree upon together. It is also important to clarify that the meetings will have some structure that is designed to ensure success of the group.

The following is the ideal structure for such a meeting:

1. **Vision**: The leader of the meeting is responsible for sharing something uplifting and positive to get the meeting off to a good start. It could be a story, an update, an article, an insight or anything else that creates an inspirational beginning to the meeting.

2. **Reviewing Goals**: Every meeting ends with each person committing to a professional and personal goal, so this is the time to simply acknowledge whether the goal was achieved or not. There is no need to have any discussion around these points. In this case, simply a statement of accomplishment or not will suffice.

3. **Questions and Feedback**: Each person gives a personal update on how things have been going regarding their chosen project and others may give feedback if requested.

4. **Ten Minute Presentation**: At each meeting, one person gets a chance to feature their own project. The

purpose here is to receive focused feedback from the entire group on any area that person may need advice on at that time.

5. **Acknowledgments**: This would be a time for anyone in the group choosing to acknowledge anyone else in the group for any reason. It could be something they did or said, or simply for being the people they are. It is important that no one feels obliged to acknowledge anyone and should be strictly voluntary and genuine.

6. **Setting Goals**: It is important that everyone in the group feel that there is real progress, rather that talk for the sake of talk. Step by step, at each meeting everyone will see incremental improvements which will serve as a motivator to continue meetings on a regular basis.

7. Team members may be a little reluctant to make a long term commitment in the beginning. To help alleviate their fears, you can simply agree on some form of trial period, and review at the end of that period. That way everyone feels comfortable that they are not making a commitment they may not be able to honor. Can you imagine what the world would be like if we had thousands of Legacy Circles a making an impact?

Connect to the World- Overview

In this section you learned the importance of cultivating gratefulness and compassion. For those that have enjoyed the fruits of their hard work, it becomes even more fulfilling to make a difference to others that might benefit from this energy, talent and wisdom. You also learned how to set up a Legacy Circles for the purpose of having an effective support system toward making an impact in the world.

The following are common questions we receive about *making an impact*:

Q. **Why is it so important to have these groups?**

A. Forming Legacy Circles is certainly not obligatory or even necessary when it comes to your own personal growth and self-mastery. However, it is quite common for people who take charge of their lives to feel a natural inclination to give back in some way. It seems that when our heart is filled with joy and inner freedom and a sense of achievement, cultivating feelings of compassion for others is a natural result. Making an impact in the world can be a big job, and so teamwork and support plays a critical role in its success. There is much more power when you have a group of like-minded individuals coming together, for the specific purpose of supporting each other in achieving their visions.

Q. **Do I really need to get into making an impact? Why can't I be happy just living my own life?**

A. This section is absolutely optional, and you can still enjoy much happiness and success without getting involved in socially responsible projects. I have only included this section because for so many people who have enjoyed much success in their lives, this has become a natural extension of their success. It is as if a natural compassionate motive for living begins to surface and the act of giving back becomes even more joyful than previous successes.

MIND GONE WILD

PART 3

Conclusion

As I mentioned at the beginning of the book, my intention here was to provide you with a unique overview and clear path to personal growth and communication mastery. That is not to say that within ninety days or so of implementing the steps, that you will have achieved nirvana and have nothing else to learn. Hopefully, we all continue to learn and grow until we die. What I am saying is that if you effectively implement the 9 steps, you will speed up and solidify true self and communication mastery more so than you would by simply gathering more information or attending inspirational talks. Finally you will be taking your awareness into "workout mode" where your inner muscles really begin to grow and impact every area of your life, consistently!

What this means is if you go through the steps, and diligently practice the exercises, you can absolutely create an amazing foundation for living a more extraordinary life in a fairly short period of time. By consistently doing the suggested exercises, you should have a much better idea of what you want out of life, discover what has been holding you back and most importantly, have access to the simple and practical step-by-step solutions toward achieving higher levels of self-mastery, inner freedom and communication mastery. To conclude it may be of some help to review the steps.

1. **Connect With Your Present** – the process begins by having the courage to look in the mirror. This self assessment is where you take time to identify your strengths and the areas you most need to work on in order to heal and grow in your professional and personal life. It is recommended that you do this exercise every few months to see your overall progress.

2. **Connect with Your Past**- We all have things from the past that continue to negatively influence our present and future. This step helps you to neutralize the power of some of these negative emotional and psychological patterns that do not serve you, and may even be sabotaging your dreams. The letting go process is divided into 2 parts. The first one has to do with letting go of any resentment, grudges or anger that you are still holding toward others. And the second one has to do with letting go of the pattern of being so self-critical - the pattern of being so hard on yourself all these years.

3. **Connect with Your Vision**- is all about crystallizing a clear vision of who you are, what you really want out of life, and cultivating a strong resolve toward achieving it. In this stage you will learn how to design an impact vision board that you will have by your side, as a constant reminder of your vision and purpose. You will also learn about the importance of having a level of determination that says, "nothing

and nobody will get me off track from achieving my desired lifestyle".

4. **Connect with Your Inner Power-** Now that you have clarified your vision and purpose, you need to begin the process of making it happen and it all starts from the inside out. It starts with your mind, emotions, intuition and tapping into your zen zone. The focus in this step is to empower yourself from the inside first, as this will set the foundation for later steps of action and effective communication. You will learn about the importance of having a calm and clear mind, a positive mindset and a heart filled with passion, enthusiasm and unconditional love. You will also learn about the importance of self acceptance, self confidence and inner power.

5. **Connect with Your Actions-** is all about implementation. True success begins on the inside but must be balanced with focused and effective action. In this stage you learned about the importance of the personal accountability system and in having a success partner to support you in accomplishing your daily and weekly goals. You also learned about the importance of prioritizing. By building your inner and outer power in steps 4 and 5 you are now in a much greater position to deal with the obstacles of life.

6. **Connect with Your Challenges-** as we continue to grow, the one thing we can count on is that sooner or later we will be confronted with obstacles and challenges. In this step we learned that we can actually embrace these challenges rather than become victims of them. We also learned that pushing through these obstacles can actually build character, mental toughness and true self mastery.

This is the closest I believe we get to experience what those in the Eastern traditions call Enlightenment. You begin to enjoy on a more consistent basis, feelings of contentment, inner peace and overall well being. You begin to experience a more stress free life without much emotional and psychological baggage. With this new found peace you are also able to access your intuitive wisdom for insights to guide every area of your life.

7. **Connect with Your Magnetism-** with all your hard work in steps 1-6, you now get a chance to enjoy the full benefits of all your labor. As the emotional and psychological turbulence melts away you now experience deep levels of inner contentment, joy and a feeling of gratitude.

8. **Connect with Others-** with all of the work you have done on your own personal growth in steps 1-7, you are now ready to communicate all these benefits with everyone around you. You learned some techniques to break the ice and connect with others more easily. You learned a technique to be a better listener and you learned about the different personality types and how to respond most effectively to each one of them. You learned that about 80% or more of your day to day communications has nothing to do with the words you speak but much more to do with the intangibles, such as humor, body language and mindset.

9. **Connect with The World-** The final step is one of giving back. You learned that the more you heal and grow as a person, the more content and confident you feel, and the more you achieve a degree of success the more you will be inclined to give back to society in some way. You learned how Legacy

Circles are one way for you to accomplish this by recognizing that in surrounding yourself with like minded people who are similarly motivated, together great things can be accomplished.

In closing, I would like thank you for taking the time to read this book and in sharing some of my life story and experiences. I hope that you at least picked up some valuable information, and more importantly find benefit in implementing some or all of the steps. Nothing would make me happier than to hear about the success stories that you experience as a result of reading this book. Please send any questions, comments or testimonials to allan@allanknight. com. My goal is to take some of the most powerful stories and share them with others through blogs or in future books. The stories can include your name or may be confidential if you prefer. The goal of sharing your success stories is to help as many people as possible learn from your experiences and breakthroughs.

As I mentioned early on in the book, I have always had a strong desire to help people and make a difference in the world. This book is really the culmination of over four decades of intense personal and professional development, and is now time to pass on my experience and wisdom to others. I wonder what's in store for the next part of my journey, I can't wait!

May this book stimulate healing, growth and success, and a deepening of all of your relationships starting with the relationship you have with yourself.

Til the next time...

Allan

About the Author

Allan Knight is an Inner Fitness and Communication Coach who has helped thousands of people around the world live more extraordinary lives. As a former zen monk and with over 25 years of coaching experience, he has the wisdom and simple formula to help us navigate through our fast paced lives with inner freedom, self confidence and communication mastery. He helps to bridge eastern philosophy with the modern world.

Over the years he has been keenly aware of the limitations of the intellect especially as it relates to personal development and interpersonal skills. As a visionary and thought leader he understood the importance of taking our awareness into action and ultimately into all of our communications both personally and professionally. His 9 step formula is a simple and comprehensive approach we can now all use in order to fast track our ability to empower and enrich our lives.

Contact Allan

Website: AllanKnight.com

Email: support@allanknight.com

Phone Toll free: 1.866.921.3330

CALM YOUR MIND

CONNECT WITH CONFIDENCE

COMMUNICATE WITH MASTERY

www.allanknight.com

33830645R00093

Made in the USA
San Bernardino, CA
28 April 2019